CHRISTOF WIECHERT

The Waldorf School

Christof Wiechert

The Waldorf School

An Introduction

Drawings by Hans Dieter Appenrodt

Verlag am Goetheanum

Note on the illustrations:
The drawings in this book were made especially for this volume by Dutch artist Hans Dieter Appenrodt. Besides their wonderful skill they also testify to real psychological understanding and a fine sense of humour – something very welcome in relation to educational themes. Appenrodt's expressive line has both depth and lightness: the designs' apparent simplicity repeatedly conjures a sense of inner joy, and the author found in them a quality that matches what he was trying to express in words.

We would like to thank Hans Dieter Appenrodt very warmly for his collaboration on this project. Copyright of the drawings remains with the author.

Translated by Matthew Barton

www.vamg.ch

Cover-Design: Wolfram Schildt, Berlin, by using a drawing
by Hans Dieter Appenrodt

Typesetting: Höpcke, Hamburg
Printing and binding: Druckhaus Nomos, Sinzheim
ISBN 978-3-7235-1539-6

Contents

Foreword by Nana Goebel 9

The Origins of Waldorf Education and Current and Future Developments 11

A First Overview of the Waldorf School 18

School buildings 18
Pupils 20
Teachers 23

Finding Out More About the Waldorf School 29

Daily school life 29
Kindergarten 29
Lower school 33
Main lessons 33
Specialist subjects:
Foreign languages 37
Handwork and craft 38
Eurythmie 41
Gymnastics and sport 42
Music 42
A glimpse of upper school life 44

The Curriculum 50

The first three school years 52
Class 4 to Class 6 56
Class 7 and 8 64

The Upper School 67

Class 9 and 10 67
Class 11 and 12 72

Pedagogy 77

Applied pedagogy 80
Temperament 82
Constitution 82
Mode of thinking 84
Imagination 85
Interests 86
Thinking versus will 88
The religious sensibility 89

Teaching Artistically 91

Teachers and their personal relationship to art 91
Using art in lessons 92
The art of education 94
Aesthetics 96

Technology and Education 98

Sources 102

Modern Challenges and Future Demands 108

External challenges 109
The relationship between state and school . . . 110
Exams and tests 110
Internal challenges 112
Structure and impulse 112
Randomness 113
Stuck in a rut 114
The social task 115

Conclusion 119

In this school, more than in another, we will need a trusting working relationship with parents if we are to progress in the right way. Our teachers will certainly be reliant on this relationship of trust with the parents of the children they teach. You see, our school is founded completely on spiritual freedom.

Rudolf Steiner
CW 298, address given at a parents evening
on 13 January 1921

Foreword

In 1919, when the first Waldorf school was founded, no written introduction to Waldorf pedagogy yet existed. Verbal accounts and descriptions had to suffice for parents, teachers, pupils and education policy-makers. At the time people were interested in trying out new ideas, in experimenting, and were willing to wait to see how things turned out before judging them. Introductory literature on the Waldorf School only began to appear in the 1970s, often with headline titles such as *Education Towards Freedom,* a bestseller by Frans Carlgren that was translated into many languages. Despite many such introductory books, still more specialist literature, and a good deal of debate in the educational mainstream, views and prejudices have remained largely unaltered. For many, Waldorf education still seems odd or enigmatic.

What therefore is the purpose of yet another introduction? With many decades of experience as a Waldorf teacher, and later as leader of the Pedagogical Section at the Goetheanum (1999 to 2009), Christof Wiechert has played a key role in broadening the horizons of this Waldorf school movement itself, posing important questions and developing its educational approach. In doing so, he has taken a hard look at sometimes too easily accepted traditions, returning to this educational movement's original roots: an understanding of child and adolescent development in terms of body, soul and spirit as the foundation of a properly individualized educational practice. This practice, too, must take full account of each specific cultural context in which it is developed. The questions of parents today, and the developmental hindrances faced by children – whether as media and advertising targets or as the focus of adult expectations – necessitate a quite new evaluation and presentation of Waldorf educational practice. In his previous books for teachers "Teaching, The Joy of Profession" (2012) and "'Solving the Riddle of the Child' – The Art of the Child Study" (2014) Christof Wiechert has enlarged on fundamental requirements which should be heeded in education in general, and Waldorf education in particular. Waldorf schools throughout the world need to reassess and reflect on their own foundations.

It is for this reason that the publishers asked Christof Wiechert to write a new introduction to Waldorf pedagogy that offers a fresh perspective to parents, critics, friends and anyone interested in the subject.

Nana Goebel

The Origins of Waldorf Education and Current and Future Developments

The period after the First World War was one of chaos and revolution in Germany. A whole nation had to come to terms with dire conditions and find a new means of livelihood. In these post-war upheavals various people tried not only to alleviate immediate suffering but also initiate new social developments which they hoped would offer a longer-term, sustainable future.

Emil Molt was one of these dynamic and active people. The socially-committed director of the Waldorf Astoria cigarette factory, he was already running a workers' educational course at his factory (in paid working hours!) and conceived the idea of establishing a school for the children of his factory workers that would offer more than the ordinary educational provision.

Molt was a student of Rudolf Steiner – which means that he sought to pursue a path of inner development and school his spiritual faculties. With a view to a better social future, many such students, members of the Anthroposophical Society, were endeavouring to support Steiner in his efforts to alleviate the miseries of the post-war period through a new structuring of society. Despite strenuous exertions by many, this impulse, known in anthroposophical circles as 'the threefold social organism', failed to make any headway.

It is irrelevant to ask whether the Waldorf schools emerged from this threefolding movement or whether they simply arose alongside it since Emil Molt was committed equally to both: to founding a new form of schooling and to social renewal. Of key importance is that Waldorf education did very rapidly begin amidst these tumultuous and chaotic circumstances at a new school in Stuttgart. The authorities gave the go-ahead for the new school because the times were so difficult. Just a few years later this window of opportunity closed again and the authorities sought to close the school by cutting the flow of pupils: permission for the new Class One was refused.

The school for the children of factory workers at the Waldorf Astoria cigarette factory opened in September 1919 in a converted restaurant in the road now called Hausmannstrasse in Stuttgart. It started with 256 pupils in 8 classes, and 12 teachers. The majority of the pupils were 'proletarian children' as they were then called, and many of them were badly malnourished due to war conditions. The school doctor, who belonged to the faculty of teachers from the beginning, had his work cut out for him. A few years later, when the school became independent of the cigarette factory context, Molt continued to ensure that the factory paid the fees for 'its' children. This new independence can be regarded as the first step towards a broader school movement: shortly after this, similar schools were founded elsewhere in

Germany. For the sake of simplicity these also became known as 'Waldorf schools'.

But the impulse to create a fundamentally different form of education not informed by state policies or religious confessions but instead emerging from and in accord with 'civil society' soon became international. As early as the 20s of the last century, and thus within a decade of the first school's founding in Stuttgart, further schools started in Germany (Essen, Hamburg, Cassel), Switzerland (Dornach, 1920), Holland (The Hague, 1923), England (London, 1925), Norway (Oslo, 1926) and America (New York, 1928).

But not long after this a curious and alarming picture emerged: whereas these schools started to spread across the globe, they gradually closed again in Germany, either voluntarily or due to state enforcement. The totalitarian Nazi state which Germany was becoming could not tolerate the Waldorf principle of guiding the developing human being towards freedom and self-determination. (In consequence of the spread of Nazi dominance across large parts of Europe, Waldorf schools that had been founded in the now occupied countries likewise had to close wherever they were identified.)

This meant that after the end of the Second World War, Waldorf schools had to be re-established and redeveloped anew amidst the ruins of war-torn Europe.

One can see therefore that truly independent schools cannot exist in totalitarian regimes, and that rejection of all subservience is a distinctive aspect of such education.

It is worth asking how the Waldorf schools would have developed in Germany if the Second World War had never happened, though it is beyond our scope to explore this further here.

Immediately after the war, the Waldorf school movement grew only slowly in Germany, the rest of Europe and other parts of the world. But in the mid to late 60s a second international growth spurt occurred. In Europe this coincided with the economic miracle as well as the criticisms of young people who sought more than material prosperity and safe careers. In this new mood of change, many Waldorf schools and kindergartens were founded in Germany and western Europe.

Something similar happened again twenty years later when perestroika and glasnost in the Soviet Union rekindled latent hopes of an unfragmented Europe. These hopes were no longer confined to young people but spread far and wide amongst people of conscience. There was great enthusiasm as the Iron Curtain finally fell and totalitarian regimes collapsed: new outlooks were suddenly conceivable and new lifestyles within reach. Since prevailing ideologies had been cemented in state schools, the urge for change and renewal extended to education. Great hopes were invested in a new, more enlightened school system, and many Waldorf schools started during this period in places that had previously been 'behind the Iron Curtain'. Parents wanted and still want a child-centred form of education, and schools with a dynamic developmental model focused not only on 'achievement' or 'performance' but also on the needs of developing children. While this desire is still apparent today across the globe, circumstances have changed somewhat. Whereas the totalitarian state once inculcated doctrines through its education system, the same now happens to some degree in democratic states, whose view of education has increasingly become results-oriented, rationally organized and selective in the Darwinian sense. The primary means used to realize these goals are pressure, and performance checks. Quality assurance is governed by inflexible testing criteria in which the pupil is seen as the 'producer' of his or her 'performance'. This leads to a reversal of aims where the school no longer serves the pupil but the pupil, instead, must secure the school's profile and standing. The task of teachers is increasingly confined, in this scenario, to supervising pupils' productivity. In my view this aptly describes the kinds of state-controlled education that now exist throughout the world.

Our understanding of democracy has therefore failed to leave education in the hands of civil society. It is the task of the state to give *everyone* access to education, but once this is secured, the actual nature of education itself, the way in which it is practised, should be left to civil society or in this case the will of parents. They ought to be free to decide what education their children receive, and how it is delivered.

The spread of Waldorf schools in this context has been driven by the unease or dissatisfaction of parents about a prepackaged and narrow model of life. Having experienced this themselves, they often wish to spare their children the same, and this has been a motivating factor in the development of Waldorf schools and kindergartens across the world. This is particularly true in the 'old world': alongside achievement-oriented education, increasing numbers of parents in Europe and the West are seeking a child-centred development model for their children's schooling.

Thus in January 2014 there were around 1200 Waldorf schools in the world and 1600 independent Waldorf kindergartens.

Recommended reading:

Murphy, Sophia Christine (2012). *The Multifaceted Life of Emil Molt (Father of the Waldorf School).* Chatham, NY: AWSNA Publications.

Gabert, Erich, and Rudolf Niederhaeuser (1998). Preface to *Faculty Meetings with Rudolf Steiner,* Volume 1. Great Barrington, MA: Anthroposophic Press.

Goebel, Nana, and Silke Heuser (2001). *The Development of Waldorf Education Including Anthroposophical Curative Education and Social Therapy.* Berlin: Friends of Waldorf Education.

Tautz, Johannes (2011). *The Founding of the First Waldorf School in Stuttgart.* Ghent, NY: Pedagogical Section Council / AWSNA Publications.

A First Overview of the Waldorf School

School buildings

In Germany, certainly, one first recognizes Waldorf schools by their distinctive premises: they often have unusual exteriors which, up to the eighties, were designed in accordance with the principles of organic architecture. Such buildings may have roofs extending beyond the walls which give them the appearance of giant mushrooms, with many slanting walls and odd-angled window frames. A large assembly hall is often situated at the centre of the school where the whole school community can gather for annual festivals, concerts or theatrical performances by different class groups, and for performances of the Christmas plays which still take place in many schools. The latter were originally conceived as a gift to the pupils and their parents from the teachers.

If the school is of a fair size, there will also be music rooms, gymnastic halls and eurythmy rooms. One may pass workshops for woodwork and metalwork, as well as art rooms. In other words, a Waldorf school needs plenty of space. Usually the kindergarten will be located at a separate site on the campus, but is an integrated part of the school community. This is partly because children of different ages grow up together and should therefore be aware of each other, but secondly because it is one of the guiding social principles of Waldorf education that all who work in its community are seen as equal, irrespective of whether they work at secondary, primary or nursery level. A kindergarten teacher or nursery nurse are just as important as a specialist secondary teacher. (In the past it was common for wages to be governed not by experience and status but by a teacher's circumstances and needs, and there are still schools that seek appropriate contemporary ways of realizing this important social principle.)

Visiting the school premises one is also struck by the coloured exterior and interior walls: subject rooms in cheerful, lively colours, the assembly hall painted in an aesthetically pleasing shade, and each classroom in its own distinctive colour. And pink curtains in the kindergarten windows! Pupil paintings and drawings hang in the corridors, and a sculpture by an upper school pupil or an art teacher may adorn the entrance to the school. Thus the whole makes an artistic and colourful impression.

Whether or not you like this or consider it beautiful is not the point. The aim here is to create an artistic and aesthetic environment for children, one in which they feel happy and at home. It is well known that sensory impressions such as shape and colour affect our unconscious sense of wellbeing – or also, depending on the nature of forms and colours, as feelings of alienation, anxiety or even aversion. Such underlying moods become lodged in children's memory and subtly colour recollections of their school days.

The premises where a child attends school for long hours over several years will become a 'second home', and so a school ought not to look like a military barracks or a nuclear power station. Actually there are some Waldorf schools in Germany that have succeeded in converting military-type buildings into cheerful, colourful and welcoming schools.

Recommended reading on the unconscious effects of shape and colour in school buildings:

Rittelmeyer, Christian (2010). The Human Body as a Resonance Organ: A Sketch of an Anthropology of the Senses, in *Research Bulletin*, Volume XV Number 2. Wilton, NH: Research Institute for Waldorf Education.

The pupils

Is there any way of recognizing Waldorf pupils as distinct from others? In earlier times pupils in Class Three and Four used to wear colourful, woolly hats they had knitted themselves, but this is no longer thought 'cool'. Yet they do still often have a distinctive openness and frankness about them. You can often seeing pupils taking musical instruments with them to school – violins, cellos, horns, trumpets, perhaps even a bassoon. And sometimes school corridors are awash with instruments, when a school orchestra is due to rehearse. When upper school pupils leave school at the end of the day, you notice their gaiety and exuberance. They are open and eager to talk, though they can also seem a tad too nonchalant and easy-going in their demeanour, perhaps even slapdash. Unfortunately, like all their contemporaries, they are media-savvy and wired up to devices, even though, in physics lessons, they are likely to have done experiments to show that microwaves from a mobile phone switched on in the classroom register on an electronic detector.

But if you have ever heard – and seen – a full upper school Waldorf choir sing together, you will have had a direct and very striking experience of undaunted young people who stand there with a wonderful presence and self-possession. There is nothing like it.

Recommended reading: research on the biographies of former Waldorf pupils:

Mitchell, David, and Douglas Gerwin (2007). *Survey of Waldorf Graduates, Phase II.* Wilton, NH: Research Institute for Waldorf Education.

Dahlin, Bo (2008). Summary of Swedish Waldorf Schools Evaluation Report, in *Survey of Waldorf Graduates, Phase III.* Wilton, NH: Research Institute for Waldorf Education.

The teachers

Is there such a thing as a typical, 'genuine' Waldorf teacher?

There used to be lots of jokes about this. A real Waldorf teacher, it was said, was always overworked and too busy to speak to you, whereas a cheerful teacher probably wasn't working hard enough!

One thing is certain: former upper school pupils know very precisely who is really a Waldorf teacher and who not. Day-in, day-out they have first-hand experience of this and, in summary, have expressed these qualities as follows: 'Someone who not only knows their subject but also knows us, is creative and flexible but also dedicated to realizing their aims. Very importantly, Waldorf teachers do not have favourites! They respond with the same respect and acknowledgement to pupils with difficulties and to the ablest in the class. Their teaching is individual, interesting, engaging and they really have something to say. But they also concern themselves with matters not directly to do with the school, for instance our personal challenges or difficulties. They show warmth, and have a depth that they rarely display but which can be felt. Many of them embody a desirable ideal for their pupils, even though the latter will be aware, at the same time, of their limitations and shortcomings.'

The picture is somewhat different in the lower school, firstly because former pupils look back to their earlier schooling from a greater distance, but also because each situation is so different in kind. What pupils remember, though, is not a particular skill their teacher possessed but his or her loving attention to them.

We can sum up their responses roughly as follows:

'Did we feel safe and protected, did we like being with the teacher for so many years? How did they draw on the board, write, do maths with us, and tell stories? Were we able to trust and share confidences with the teacher, did we feel understood by him or her? And when we were older, did he or she grow with us too, or instead stay stuck, somehow, speaking to us when we were eleven as if we were still nine? Was the teacher warm-hearted, knowing how to relate to different temperaments and characters? And when we were older, in Class 7 and 8, could he or she fully satisfy our thirst for knowledge, or did things get a bit 'thin on the ground'? Did the teacher teach artistically and imaginatively, or was there too much boring repetition?'

While scarcely acknowledged by public opinion, the work of nursery teachers is becoming increasingly important. Developments at the end of the 20th century, and still more at the beginning of the 21st, have made it harder to discern generally applicable laws of development in children. Among other things this means that classical 'school readiness'[1] now requires a longer process of preparation. Early childhood development leading to learning readiness is now complicated by a variety of factors that have changed in the past 25 years.

1 In Germany, formal schooling does not start until age 6.

But a great deal still depends on a successful nursery education period, and kindergarten practitioners have to ground their charges in the healthy, basic aptitudes of daily life so that they can engage in formal learning when the time comes. For this reason, the Waldorf schools work closely with nurseries and kindergartens to ensure this happens.

These are ideal pictures, focused on the educational nurturing of fundamental human capacities, and it is worth characterizing such ideals to offer interested readers a basic orientation from the outset. We will return to this theme later. Such pictures also need to be enlarged by a description of the wide range of specialist subjects – music, foreign languages, gymnastics and sport, gardening, eurythmy, craft and handwork, IT, metalwork and so forth. All these subjects and the teachers responsible for them, are dedicated, ideally, to the same fundamental aims. In addition, in the upper school, there will be specialist teachers in maths, physics, chemistry, biology, geography, history, art history, language and literature and, not least, drama. The school, after all, should be a cosmos offering all kinds of paths of entry into the world.

If we continue this ideal characterization, we ought not to forget, either, that the teachers are united by a spiritual bond woven in weekly meeting where collegiate attention is given to the development model at the heart of the school. Here space is given to questions about individual children and their difficulties, with efforts to understand and help them. In the faculty of teachers everything will be done to nurture each pupil's healthy all-round development. In these meetings, therefore, efforts are made to shape the whole school environment together so that each colleague develops mutual respect and awareness for every other.

In his 'Letters on the Education of the Human Race', Lessing offered three striking pictures of authority that give us insight into the educational process. The first is an old-fashioned, hierarchical one: above us stands the law and then, further down, the prophets, below which live human beings. If we act in conformity with the law, we are 'pleasing to God'. In the second picture the law descends and becomes embodied in a human being. Now humankind lives in imitation, the 'Imitatio Christi' of Thomas à Kempis. In the third picture, the law is incorporated into each separate individual: people become self-responsible and autonomous. (The Greek word 'auto-nomos' means 'to give the law unto oneself'.)

All these three levels of education still exist today. But perhaps there is now a fourth, too, that we should consider. Is it possible that the law now no longer just lives in each individual separately but that the next developmental stage embodies a new level of interaction between people, the interplay of many to create a greater work – as Goethe suggests in his fairytale, *The Green Snake and the Beautiful Lily*?

Is this the underlying reason why Steiner placed key importance on the *collaborative* endeavours of teachers at Waldorf schools? He cultivated this very rigorously in the meetings he held with the teachers at the first school in Stuttgart; and this was also why it was decided not to have a school principal or directorate but instead entrust educational responsibility to the whole faculty together.

Today many institutions, including Waldorf schools, have to reinvent themselves after a certain period of development, and it is far from easy to renew social forms in a way that accommodates the changing nature of these institutions. Many schools find it difficult to realize these social forms of collaboration in a way appropriate for our times.

Recommended reading:

Lessing, Gotthold Ephraim: *The Education of the Human Race*, translated by Fred W. Robertson, M.A. London, C.K. Paul & Co., 1881.

Goethe, Johann Wolfgang von (1775-2006): *The Fairytale of the Green Snake and the Beautiful Lily*, Phanes Press 1993; in particular this passage, spoken by the man with the lamp: 'I do not know whether I can help; one alone does not help but only he who joins with others at the right time.'

Schieren, Jost (2012). The Concept of Learning in Waldorf Education, in *Research Bulletin,* Volume XVII Number 2. Wilton, NH: Research Institute for Waldorf Education.

Schieren, Jost (2014). The Spiritual Dimension of Waldorf Education, in *Research Bulletin,* Volume XIX Number 1. Wilton, NH: Research Institute for Waldorf Education.

Finding Out More About the Waldorf School

Daily school life

As in all schools, pupils stream towards their school from all directions. Since the Waldorf school may sometimes have a large catchment area, school buses and cars will often bring the children. Many older children come unaccompanied. A crowd of them swarm into the kindergarten, lower school and upper school buildings. It is an unwritten rule that teachers receive their charges with a handshake at the door of the classroom: a first, morning greeting.

Kindergarten

Kindergarten children play freely for a while until their teacher gathers them together and starts a prepared activity, which may vary widely. For instance, they might build a playhouse, make something for Advent, go for a walk or spend a longer time playing, either indoors or out. The teacher will, at all events, try to create a 'breathing' sequence to the day: both guided and independent activity, play alongside 'work' (painting, laying the table for break-time, clearing up and tidying, washing dishes etc.). In fact, anything that initiates imitation and purposeful actions is possible and welcome. And of course there will be storytime with a simple fairytale.

The toys available are largely made of natural materials, not because of some misguided nostalgia but simply to convey as many diverse sensory impressions as possible. A shell feels different from a stone, and the latter different from a pinecone or plastic ball. Care and cultivation of the senses is given great importance especially because our culture tends to be impoverished in sensory experience. Much scope is given to the sense of touch, movement and life (sense of wellbeing or its opposite, feelings of hunger, the urge to spend time outside) which are called the 'lower senses' and are fundamental for children's healthy sense of their own physicality, of being at home in themselves. Kindergarten life is wonderfully free-flowing and embedded in community which the children as yet are not consciously aware of: for them everything is still so new and immediate; they live in the here and now.

Play and imitation are the great teachers at this age. Imitation informs (purposeful) movements and activity, and play offers creative engagement with the world. All organized learning is dispensed with in favour of these foundational activities. Because of the urbanization of our culture, some kindergarten teachers, by agreement with parents, spend a whole day each week in the park or woods. In many schools the little ones can now stay

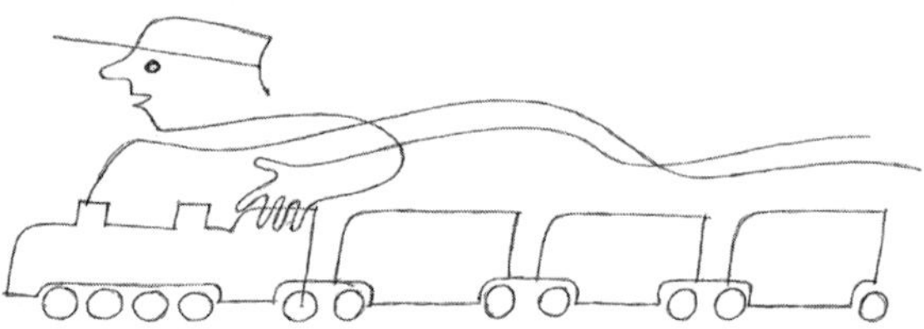

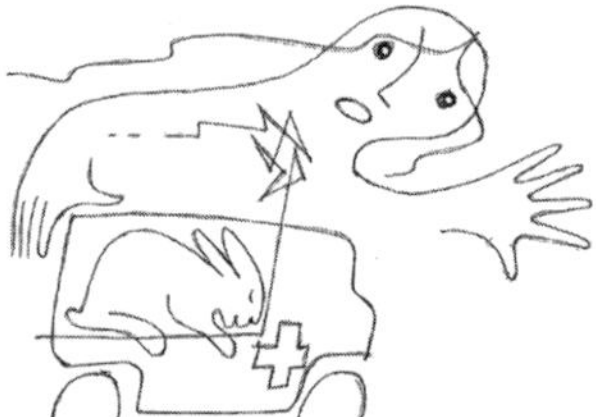

all day, in which case they will have a nap after lunch and then carry on playing either indoors or out – always supervised of course – until it is home time.

Lower school

Arriving in their classrooms in the morning, the children are welcomed by their classteacher, and unpack their schoolbags or satchels. After a song, a brief narrative or story, choral recitation of a poem or some other warm-up (clapping a rhythm, mental arithmetic) the school day begins with the 'morning verse'. This offers a blessing on the children's work but is not a prayer as such. It focuses attention on what is to come, to support and stimulate learning. In this first period of the day we encounter a distinctive aspect of the Waldorf School in an unusual form of lesson.

Main lessons

Long before anyone had thought of 'project teaching' Rudolf Steiner conceived the idea of the 'main lesson' – which means that the first two hours of the day (in some schools just 100 minutes) are given over to the same subject for three or four weeks.

After this comes break-time, followed by subject lessons. After lunch there are further specialist subjects, if possible of a more artistic and craft-based kind, often in double lessons. The subjects taught in the morning are devoted to things requiring regular practice: foreign languages, eurythmy, practice of English or maths, while afternoon lessons tend to be such things as handwork, craft, singing and music. For older pupils there will be sport and gardening in the afternoon, as well as drama, woodwork and smithying.

In other words, ideally the day starts with absorbing new material (main lesson) then subjects requiring practice, and in the afternoon more artistic and craft-based activity. If this proves largely feasible we speak of a 'healthy' timetable.

Thus main lesson belongs in the morning, and the somewhat longer teaching period given to this each day enables pupils and teachers to engage in a deeper way with various subjects and look at them from a wide range of different perspectives. In the early years of formal schooling, the subjects are not yet clearly divided or distinguished. Reading, writing and arithmetic are not confined to the main lessons but are continually being practised. But from Class 3 and 4 the real main lesson periods begin, and these continue to the end of schooling. As well as reading, writing and arithmetic these main lessons encompass geography, history, mathematics, geology, chemistry, astronomy, geometry, physics, biology (zoology, botany, human biology) and, later on in the upper school, literature and the history of literature, art history, geometry and stereometry, embryology, social sciences, economics and computer studies. This broad range of subjects expresses and embodies the wealth of the culture in which we live. In the view of Waldorf educators, schools ought to mirror the richness and diversity of the culture of which they are a part, and not only a more classical canon of subjects.

The main lesson makes it possible to explore, at leisure, diverse aspects and offshoots of a subject, and allows pupils to engage fully with the material. One very clear advantage of this form of teaching is that shared exploration of a subject can continue each day afresh over a longer period. It is well known that, after a night' sleep, what was introduced the day before is present to pupils in a more vivid way than the day before. (Brain research has shown that this 'assimilation' of content – and thus its understanding and application – occurs during the night following its first teaching in both the declarative [explicit] and procedural [implicit] memory.) This learning rhythm extending through many days and nights underpins the demonstrable effectiveness of main lesson teaching.

Pupils work through what they are learning in self-created **main lesson books** which (from a certain age onwards) are provided for every subject and record key aspects of learning in both copied and self-composed texts, along with carefully and richly illustrated motifs. This will depend of course on the capacity and talents of each pupil. In our era of never-ending rationalization and rationality, attention to this aspect of the main lesson, and enjoyment of it, may not always be something every teacher succeeds in conveying, and somewhat 'threadbare' main lesson books can result. At the same time there are also many former Waldorf pupils who guard their old main lesson books as a real treasure, and reminder of a rich learning experience.

We can regard these main lesson books, in fact, as a kind of reversal of the textbook idea: pupils themselves compose what they are learning. In a sense the idea of the 'portfolio' of work originates here.

A further fundamental principle of Waldorf pedagogy is that a teacher should create her **methodology** from her own resources. If Waldorf education is to be worthy of the name, account must be taken of this challenging requirement. This means that teachers engage so fully and individually with each subject that they really make it their own: they themselves become the medium through which it is conveyed to pupils, rather than resorting to a ready text or methodology. Teachers allow each subject to inspire them, so that they can then shape, convey and explain it through their own insights. This gives a sense of immediate connection to the subject through the person of the teacher, rather than a second-hand imparting of what others have determined or advised.

The reproach that Waldorf Schools too often favour 'teaching from the front' must be countered by saying that this art of education has always drawn on a wide diversity of methods. However, we can also recognize how challenging it has been to develop this individual freedom of methodology, and why sometimes an impoverishment of teaching method has arisen – currently something that is being strenuously reviewed and re-energized.

Main lesson teaching:

Avison, Kevin (1995). *A Handbook for Waldorf Class Teachers.* Edinburgh: Floris Books.

D'Aleo, Michael, and Stephen Edelglass (1999). *Sensible Physics Teaching.* Austin, TX: Parker Courtney Press.

Foreign languages

From Class 1 (age 6-7) onwards, one or two languages are taught in two or three lessons a week. Today there is no longer any need to justify early foreign language teaching, although it was revolutionary when the first Waldorf school was founded.

At this young age children learn and absorb a foreign language in the same way that they learned their mother tongue: not through intellectual instruction but by imitation. In the lower classes therefore these lessons are entirely oral, based on simply speaking to one another, alongside the learning of verses, poems and songs. This is hard work for the teacher but the only way to develop facility in a foreign language at that age. This kind of teaching asks for versatility and ability from teachers, often in many different classes and age groups. Success here is enhanced if a (skilful) teacher can teach the same group over several years.

Foreign language teaching:

Kiersch, Johannes (1997). *Language Teaching in Steiner/Waldorf Schools: Rudolf Steiner's Concept of an Integrated Approach to Language Teaching.* Edinburgh: Floris Books.

Forrer, Elena, et al, eds. (2000). *Senderos: Teaching Spanish in Waldorf Schools.* Chatham, NY: AWSNA Publications.

Querido, Rene (1987). A Creative Approach to Foreign Languages, in *Creativity in Education: The Waldorf Approach.* San Francisco: H. S. Dakin.

Handwork and craft

Long before neuroscience discovered that intelligence is nurtured when children learn manual skills, handwork was an integral part of the Waldorf curriculum from Class 1 onwards – both for boys and girls (an astonishing idea in 1919). It is wonderful to see Class 1 children learning to knit: the concentration they bring to the task and the pride when they master it. With this new skill in their command they start making all kinds of things, such as stuffed animals, hats in bright colours, recorder bags and oven gloves. The children love these lessons.

Especially in handwork, once fingers have learned these skills, the little ones love to talk, and tell anything that comes into their minds quite freely. If you want to know more about a child, it is a good idea to visit a handwork lesson.

Craft lessons are added to the curriculum from Class 5 onwards. Children work with wood, learning to carve concave and convex forms, and besides manual dexterity they start to apply both muscle power and the capacity to form material. In middle school (Class 6 –8) these subjects are significantly developed. In handwork the pupils learn to use sewing machines to create their own clothes, and in craft they do basket weaving and carpentry. Later, in the upper school, this can be extended further into smithying, copperware and metalwork. In some Waldorf schools one finds silversmith workshops and computer laboratories as well. In other words, there is a wide range of craftwork on offer and usually the only question is how to accommodate all this in the timetable and maintain a healthy balance between cognitive and practical learning.

Handwork and craft:

Mitchell, David, and Patricia Livingston (1999). *Will-*

Developed Intelligence: Handwork & Practical Arts in the Waldorf School — Elementary through High School. Fair Oaks, CA: AWSNA Publications.

James, Van (2014). *Drawing with Hand, Head, and Heart: A Natural Approach to Learning the Art of Drawing.* Great Barrington, MA: SteinerBooks.

Spence, Roswitha (2012). *Clothing the Play: The Art and Craft of Stage Design.* Chatham, NY: AWSNA Publications.

Auer, Arthur (2001). *Learning about the World through Modeling: Sculptural Ideas for School and Home.* Fair Oaks, CA: AWSNA Publications.

Eurythmy

This is an art of movement taught once a week in the lower classes and twice a week from Class 5 onwards. In some Waldorf schools, secondary age pupil do eurythmy project weeks and eurythmy certificates too. Sometimes class plays include eurythmy – for instance a sea voyage can be beautifully depicted in eurythmy. As conceived by Steiner, this form of movement gives visible, embodied form to words and tones: visible music and poetry. As a school subject it has an integrative and harmonizing effect, helping the 'upper' faculties of thinking and feeling to engage fully with the 'lower' ones of action, will, movement and bodily intention. Eurythmy performances by adolescents can be very striking and moving.

Bardt, Sylvia (2008). *Eurythmy: A Creative Force in Humanity*. Fair Oaks, CA: AWSNA Publications.

Gymnastics and sport

In this realm too, the Waldorf School goes its own way, especially in the form of Bothmer gymnastics devised by the first gymnastics teacher at the Waldorf school, Fritz Bothmer (1883-1941). Steiner asked him to develop movement sequences with more emphasis on movement and dynamic rather than mere muscle power. Ordinary gymnastics are also included in the curriculum as long as the timetable and premises allow it.

In many countries, the Class 5 groups meet once a year for their 'Olympic Games'. As in Ancient Greece, not only the swiftest and strongest are lauded, but those too who move with beauty and elegance.

McMillan, Jaimen (2014). Still Moving: Image and Imagination. Mechanicville, NY: Spacial Dynamics Institute.

Music

Music is intrinsic to life. Whether or not one is 'musical', it is an important expressive means and way of connecting with inner feeling experience. Shakespeare knew this when he wrote, in *The Merchant of Venice*,

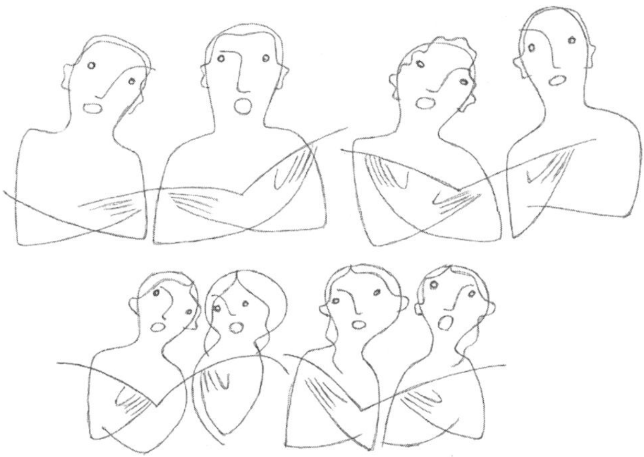

'The man that hath no music in himself / Nor is not moved with concord of sweet sounds / Is fit for treasons, stratagems, and spoils ...'

From Class I onwards singing skills are nurtured, either by a class teacher if she is able to do this or by a music teacher. If possible all children should try to learn a musical instrument, and practise in instrumental ensembles. Later on they can see if they want to continue and take this further or not. Singing however continues to the end of their school days.

Often schools will have an upper school choir, and this is also an excellent thing for social interaction since music is a social art: music always requires an audience. A mixed-age upper school choir is also an opportunity to work with others artistically and socially in the preparation of a concert. However deep the crises of puberty, involvement in a choral concert at Christmas will make a deep and harmonizing impression on a young person's sensibility. Such experiences stay in the memory as a golden resource for the future. The same is true of orchestral work in the lower or upper school, or a brass band in middle school.

Music education:

Masters, Brien, ed. (1987). *The Waldorf Song Book.* Edinburgh: Floris Books.

Barnes, Diane Ingraham (2013). *Music Through the Grades: In the Light of the Developing Child.* Hillsdale, NY: Adonis Press.

A glimpse of upper school life (age 15 onwards)

Like the younger children, upper school pupils still gather in their own classroom each morning and are welcomed there with a handshake by their specialist teachers. And yet the whole mood has changed, along with the nature of the teaching relationship and mode of teaching. Now the main lesson teacher is a specialist in her subject; and when one main lesson period has ended after a few weeks, a different specialist arrives for the next. The pupils no longer have a class-teacher, and the group's cohesion is based more on their own social interactions and the supervision of their class mentor or guardian. In Class 9 this has to develop as a new departure, and this year can therefore sometimes be a little tumultuous. But upper school teachers are ready for this and know how to calm things down with a little humour, and, if necessary, gently restrain some of their charges' more excessive outfits and apparel.

It is a basic principle that all pupils attend all subject lessons, including maths, physics and chemistry. The range of subjects we referred to earlier is part of a whole developmental trajectory that all can benefit from. A simple example can illustrate this: Children in Class 6 (age 11/12) do not yet have the emotional maturity to grasp the implications and context of a revolution – say the French or Russian – and therefore they would get no more from studying this than external historical facts. But they do find the emergence and development of the Roman Empire and Roman culture very engaging. By Class 9, pupils' own mental and emotional life is in something like revolutionary turmoil and they immediately grasp the revolutions of history. Thus the Waldorf curriculum tries to follow and reflect general developmental phases in the children themselves.

The selection and differentiation of skills and abilities is postponed for as long as possible in Waldorf schools. Preparation for exams is regarded as an important yet subsidiary goal of schooling, and not its primary concern. Of greater importance is to offer a fully lived and experienced curriculum addressing all aspects of the developing child. In absorbing and assimilating this diverse provision, pupils also take exams in their stride. Here there may be tensions between the expectations of parents, society and pupils themselves, and the emphases of Waldorf pedagogy. But by their very identity, Waldorf schools cannot see themselves only as an institution geared to exams. These are necessary today, but only have an indirect connection with real learning and education.

Following main lesson in the morning, upper school pupils attend specialist lessons which, in the higher grades, will include work that prepares them for exams.

In science subjects, teachers try to complement examination requirements with more wide-ranging reflections on science – a real challenge! They believe that other scientific paradigms should be introduced besides commonly prevailing positivist and reductionist outlooks. Phenomenology offers a rich field of study, and, for instance, Goethe's theory of colours is studied alongside that of Newton. Modern physics is taught but also questioned, thus awakening in pupils existential questions about how we see the world and what it really is.

In asking such questions we are also asking who and what we are as human beings. It is excellent for adolescent pupils to focus not only on the biological human being but to greatly broaden these horizons with enquiries into human nature.

During these years, while chemistry seeks to convey tangible understanding of the world's organic and inorganic foundations, biology and anthropology examine the nature of human existence.

Traditional history lessons are likewise extended through actual practice of the 'symptomatic mode of observation' recommended by Steiner. Pupils are helped to 'read' phenomena in a way that shows them to be symptomatic of a whole phase of historical development. Very broad horizons can open up here, at the same time giving pupils a stance with which to observe their own lives and its occurrences in an unbiased way.

In Class 9, in literature studies, the theme of humour has a freeing, lightening effect that can counter the subjective sufferings undergone at that age; and in Class 12 the reading of selected texts from world literature can confirm young people as they grow surer of their identity. In the intervening years there will be main lesson on poetics, the great works of European culture, and a study of Wolfram von Eschenbach's *Parzival*, with its deep quest for self-knowledge.

These developmental trajectories apply also to mathematics, beginning in Class 9 with equations, combinatorial analysis and a first look at statistics, and ending in Class 12 with an elementary engagement with integral value and differential value calculations. Between this beginning and ending lie whole worlds that are not just the basis for a career in mathematics but offer aspects of a fully rounded general education.

The same is true of the other subjects, which include global economics, geology, embryology and cosmology. For instance, land surveying in mathematics leads in Class 11 into the art of cartography. In other words, pupils learn to draw a map that corresponds to mathematical and geometrical rules.

Then too pupils study art history and music history. The curriculum has universal aspects, offering a great wealth of themes and a synthesis of human culture. But to balance all this, practical arts and crafts continue: drawing, painting, modelling, perhaps sculpture; and one may ask how all this can be fitted into so few years. And in fact the timetable may become overloaded (since there are also work placements, exam work and drama projects to be fitted in) if teaching colleagues do not work closely with each other; in which case the curriculum will not fully achieve what it should, which is to prepare young people to determine their own life and take up their creative place in the world. Yet often one is astonished to find that these young people do assimilate everything and cope with all the demands, with great energy and enthusiasm. The curriculum is very rich and varied, reflecting humanity's ongoing conversation with itself and the world. Every young person has a right to this kind of preparation for life.

Recommended further reading:

Schubert, Ernst (2009). *Mathematics Lessons for the Sixth Grade.* Fair Oaks, CA: AWSNA Publications.

Schubert, Ernst (2009). *The First Steps in Proven Geometry: For the Upper Elementary Grades.* Fair Oaks, CA: AWSNA Publications.

Ulin, Bengt (1991). *Finding the Path: Themes and Methods for the Teaching of Mathematics in a Waldorf School.* Wilton, NH: AWSNA Publications.

Maier, Georg (2011). *An Optics of Visual Experience.* Hillsdale, NY: Adonis Press.

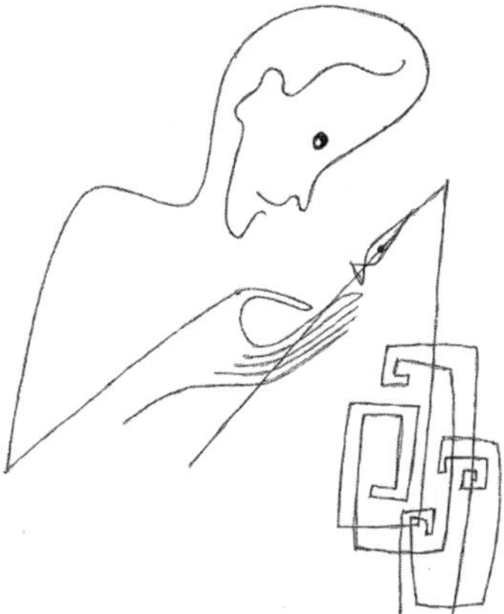

The Curriculum

The founder of the first Waldorf School, Emil Molt, asked Rudolf Steiner to draw up plans for the school, devise a curriculum and formulate a modern pedagogical approach. He also asked him to establish the school practically, in other words to appoint teachers and act as the school's director as far as possible.

Steiner conceived a curriculum that differs from others in that it is drawn from the nature of child development itself and aims to correspond to and stimulate this development. In other words, what children learn is not dictated by a learning requirement imposed on them externally – subjects that must be learned, capacities that must be developed – but on what *they really benefit* by learning and experiencing at any moment of their development. To subscribe to this view one has to share the belief, firstly, that children do actually develop, and secondly that it is important *when* they learn something.

There are of course other views of these things, for instance that every child develops individually and should therefore himself decide what he wishes to learn (as practised in 'free schools' such as A.S. Neill's Summerhill). Some also think it does not matter when one learns something, and that basically we can learn whatever we need to at any point in life, as long as the methodology used to teach it is skilfully applied (as practised in the constructivist approach). Others believe it does not matter what you teach as long as the subjects are rationally organized. These are just some of the approaches that show the rich diversity of educational methods available and enshrined in a democratic society. Ultimately parents should be able to decide what form of education they wish for their offspring.

Waldorf schools recognize generally apparent developmental stages that all children and people pass through to a more or less equal degree. *As a rule* we learn to stand upright before we walk, and our thinking develops from the capacity to speak. All children become 'ready' for formal school learning, some more rapidly than others; and in the same way all pass through certain psychological changes around the age of eight or nine, and physical and bodily changes, as well as psychological ones, at puberty. Boys pass through these stages in a different way from girls; and yet by the age of eighteen, young people all more or less reach a stage approaching adulthood. In Waldorf schools there is a conviction that these developments unfold in perceptible rhythms even if there are also considerable deviations from the 'norm'.

From birth to the end of schooling, therefore, we all take a similar path whether this proceeds in a straighter trajectory or embarks on diversions and bypasses. The overall direction remains the same and we all become adults.

The curriculum corresponds to this overall developmental trajectory. We can see it as a road that spirals ever higher up a mountain, and at the top offers a panoramic view of the world.

What is the nature of this road? We can regard school readiness as a phase in the child's development at which a first stage has been attained in growth and development which, as it continues, also alters in quality: as growth forces continue, different faculties are also *released* to facilitate a form of learning less directly dependent on daily life. Alongside learning through play and life itself, therefore, direct learning now becomes possible too.

The first three school years

In these years (from age 6/7 onwards) the children learn to read, write, count and do arithmetic. They learn (usually) two foreign languages, and handwork helps them develop fine motor skills (which has a beneficial effect on general intelligence). They are introduced to music through singing, eurythmy addresses their whole motor and movement ability, they learn writing from drawing and form drawing, and in painting they learn to handle and balance colours. They listen to stories and tales: fairy-tales in Class 1, fables and legends in Class 2, and Old Testament stories in Class 3.

One peculiarity of this approach is that children learn to read from what they themselves have written, and so write before they have learned to read! (Thus

motor skills – in evolutionary terms an older capacity – support the more recent capacity of reading.) Distinctive also is the fact that all four processes are taught and practised in maths simultaneously, rather than adding first, and this at the same time relates to and addresses the 'four temperaments'. Simultaneous application of these four processes allows the diverse nature of numbers to be effectively grasped. If, say, we consider the number 24 in terms of addition, subtraction, multiplication and division, we can recognize what a 'rich' number this is. Alongside arithmetical skills, a qualitative sense of the numbers develops too. The scope of numbers involved does not have to be small. In the same way that writing is developed from drawing, arithmetic is developed from handling objects – beans, stones, conkers – in tangible situations.

The children also make initial forays into experience of their environment. The surrounding world is addressed in a way that gives a sense of these surroundings being ensouled – for instance a snowdrop will have a conversation with a tall, dark fir tree. A story on this theme might run as follows: The fir tree laughs at the little slip of a thing down there between its roots, which will only be there a little while. But the snowdrop says: 'I may be small, but look at the lovely white flower I have brought forth in this cold weather. You with your great trunk and strong branches have no flower to be seen. And the fir tree falls silent, reflectively.'

A simple example like this can show how the Waldorf curriculum engages with, and responds to the magical-moral worldview of young children. At the same time little narratives like this stimulate thinking about relationships between different things in the world.

The whole of Class 3 is infused with a kind of summer evening mood. The purer innocence of childhood is drawing to an end, a little like a farewell from paradise.

Naturally teachers, in particular the class teacher, ensure that learning aims are attained, and these are outlined to parents at the start of each year.

The teachers as a whole base their teaching aims both on the general Waldorf curriculum and on its individualization in each school.

Class 4 to Class 6

During the course of Class 4, a subtle change become perceptible in the children. Some time around the age of nine, their view of the world changes. In the first three years, they still inhabit a 'magical reality', without as yet a clear division between subject and object. They often still believe in Father Christmas and the Easter Hare. If, say, they can hold their breath till they reach the next street light, then... something they wish for will happen. Hitherto the class teacher will be seen in a certain aura of wonder; but suddenly a child notices that she has a pimple on her nose! This can be slightly shocking for them. A teacher is just a person, and the world becomes a more mundane place. Insecurities can arise at this age, with brief phases of anxiety and little encroachments upon their previously intact and trusting relationships with key people in their lives. The openness with which they encounter the world is likely to be affected.

These are subtle changes, like fluctuations of mood, rather than radical transformations; but children at this age need a little additional attentiveness. Sometimes these changes, which are often hard to discern, only arise towards the end of Class 4. They are perfectly normal and no cause for greater concern.

The Waldorf curriculum responds to these inner changes in a very decided way. The narrative material for this year turns once more (after the biblical Creation of the world in Class 3) to another creation myth, but now drawn from Nordic mythology. Why does it do so? In these Scandinavian myths we find a vivid portrayal of the end of the communal life between the gods and men, which is, at the same time, nothing other than the end of a magical view of the world, a twilight of the gods. Henceforth people must manage in the world by their own resources and the gods are no longer available to help. (In Class 5, this theme continues, showing, in Greek mythology, how humankind learns to develop autonomously and independently of the gods and create human culture. By this point the human being stands balanced between above and below, between Olympus and the underworld, as depicted for instance in the demi-gods Heracles and Prometheus and, increasingly in independent human figures such as Perseus, Ariadne and cunning Odysseus.)

Apart from these pictures in mythology, the inner changes at this time are reflected also in fractions, form drawings which now involve more complex intersecting forms – as in Celtic manuscripts such as the Book of Kells and Irish grave stones – and in an engagement with grammar, and thus the structure of sentences (syntax). Round and part singing involves holding one's own voice against others, and in handwork cross-stitch continues the theme of intersection, at the same time revealing, for the first time, a pronounced difference between top and bottom: the upper side of cross-stitch looks quite different from the underside, like two different but related worlds.

A new subject is introduced at this time: biology, which is focused initially on the animal realm. The emphasis here is on comparing the human being with animals and discerning important differences. One poem written by a class teacher goes as follows:

The animal's lot is mostly this:
With eager eye and lowered head
To find the tastiest leaves of grass
Or other stomach-fodder: to be fed.

Free and upright, his head held high
The human being walks on earth.
Free of the ground his hands can ply
Their trade, and praise Creation's wealth.

After a general outline of these differences between man and animals, the class will study certain animals in more detail. The aim at this stage is not to develop expertise in zoology, but to characterize the qualities of an animal so that pupils gain a sense of essential characteristics and 'gestures' in a particular species, better even than by observing them in the zoo. The first Waldorf school doctor, Eugen Kolisko, once summed up the lion succinctly in this main lesson by saying: 'The lion is an animal that makes a promise in front that it does not keep behind.' Not only is this correct in morphological terms but also physiologically: the lion's digestive tract is astonishingly 'thin', as is its excrement. Thus efforts are made by the teacher to describe animals in a way that show diverse one-sided aspects of human functions, nervous system, breathing and metabolism, and also the beauties of these 'modifica-

tions'. In a presentation of children's work, the children may then greatly enjoy depicting some of these animal qualities in a 'circus show'.

The geography main lesson is also something new in Class 4. This engages with the geography and related history of the children's immediate locality, leading to a lively interest in their surroundings and its past. In Class 5 follows the first history main lesson, which carefully introduces the transition from a mythological to an historical view of things. However, this main lesson does not start with, say, Neanderthal man, but with the first indications of a consciously developing culture in ancient India.

Fractions in Class 4 lead in Class 5 to decimal fractions. The grammar of parts of speech in Class 4 is extended into sentence structure in Class 5. Where the narrative content of Class 4 finds its dramatic ending in the twilight of the gods (and the bereft human being as a reflection of the child's increasing sense of loneliness), the Hellenic sun casts its light over Class 5. A new (self-) assurance is found and is reflected in a more balanced relationship between the human being and the world, as embodied in classical times. While zoology continues, the focus in Class 5 is more on the world of plants, and botany is added to the range of subjects.

In fact, if we survey the whole period from Class 1 to Class 8, from age 6 to age 14, we find this year of Class 5 to be the most balanced and harmonious.

A fine custom in Waldorf schools is to start the day with a spoken recitation, usually called the 'morning verse' (which is not intended as a prayer). There is a morning verse for the Classes 1 through to 4; and then a different one from Class 5 onwards, which conveys a sense of how we can appropriate and engage with the world in learning and work.

There is often a distinct change in children in Class 5: their interests flourish, their gifts and talents become more apparent, and their temperaments are consolidated.

Class 6 reaffirms all that has so far been learned but gives it stronger, more solid foundations. Pupils take pride in their increasing mastery of various subjects, which gives them a sense of being at home in an ever-broadening world. Here I will offer just four examples of how the curriculum seeks to widen and enlarge the children's horizons. Geography leads into mineralogy (not yet geology proper); sciences start with a main lesson on physics; the narrative content turns to the Roman era and culture, and thus to legal ideas and the principle of equality; and in mathematics, while everything previously learned goes on being practised, new processes are introduced of a commercial nature such as interest calculation, the setting of purchase and sale prices, and the calculation of profit and loss in percentages. Interest calculations prefigure the introduction of algebra in Class 7.

Of these years, Classes 6, 7 and 8 it is worth saying the following: it is always easier to hasten development rather than keep it measured, and really work through all that is needed. The great biologist Portmann knew this: he compared animal and human development, and concluded that the former tended to speed up (propulsive) while the latter was predicated on slower maturation (retardation).

In Class 7 and 8 it is relatively easy to greatly hasten the children's development towards puberty. It is a greater art to keep pupils instead in pre-pubescence and allow them to mature slowly through a form of teaching oriented to broad overviews and holism. Specialism will come into its own in the subsequent years. In Class 7 and 8 we can still stay with a sense of larger 'gestures' and broader perspectives. Gradually, over this period, young people dispense with the need to be so closely directed and accompanied.

In psychological terms the pupils at this age are no longer children but nor are they yet adults by a long chalk. Really they do not need the class teacher any more in the same way, yet they seem helpless without

her. Class 7 pupils seem a little like calves: charming to see and pat, but awkward in their interactions. They like thinking of their teacher as a friend and pal, but she must still ensure that all runs smoothly.

Here the curriculum helps pupils to 'grow up'. Besides physics, chemistry is introduced, and alongside arithmetic, proper algebra and geometry (which began in Class 6 with freehand geometry). Biology which has until now been concerned with zoology and botany is significantly expanded to address human anatomy (skeleton and muscular system), complemented in physics by general laws of mechanics, with an account of levers and pulleys. A year after this (Class 8), biology studies more functional aspects such as metabolic processes, circulatory processes and sensory functions.

In geography so far, the emphasis has been on Europe, but this is now enlarged to consider the world's continents. In Class 7 history examines the great voyages of discovery from the Renaissance onwards, and in Class 8 the history of industrialization. The steam engine, turbines, internal combustion engine, electric power systems, radio, television, and computer: these have altered the world more radically than all wars put together. During these years, still, foreign languages, handwork, singing, craft and gardening continue to be part of the curriculum.

It should be apparent from this (incomplete) account of the subjects taught how the curriculum is not only of great scope and richness but also traces a path of development extending ever further out into the world and towards an objective grasp of it. To be a class teacher over this span of time makes great demands on a teacher's general knowledge and ability to change and learn on the job. But where this proves successful, the developmental trajectory is a wonderful time of growth and enrichment.

The last two years of this period, however they are handled by individual schools, mark both a culmination of, and farewell to childhood.

Class 7 and 8

Some schools introduce a 'middle school' at this age. This means that the class teacher from Class 1 to Class 6 is succeeded by another who has particular skills with this age group. Subject teachers may also change now. (See the chapter on 'Modern Challenges and Future Demands'.)

But however these school years are handled, the curriculum always follows the pedagogical principle of echoing and responding to the developing child.

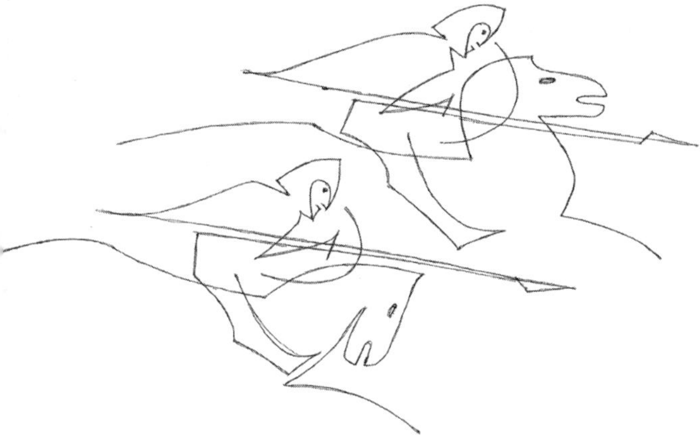

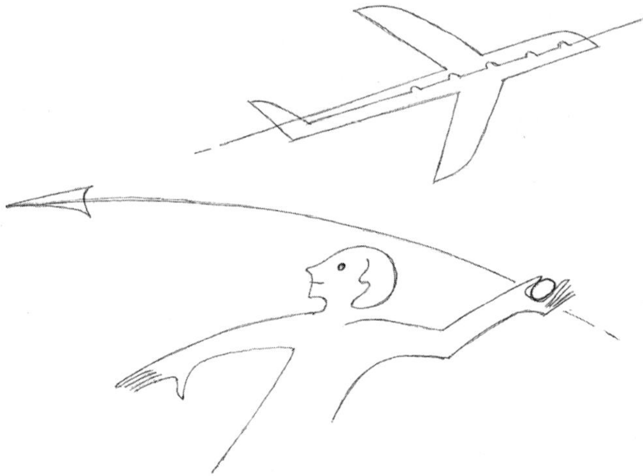

The Upper School

Class 9 and 10

Psychologists debate whether human development is continuous or if it runs in phases and – if the latter is true – whether there are gaps or even breaks between the phases. Currently it is thought that we develop in a continuous, strictly individualistic way, without phases, and that every child and every human being is unique as regards genetic disposition and socialization. Likewise, our capacity to learn, it is thought, is not tied to any specific age. In this view, children themselves determine when and how they can or wish to learn things. This is the view currently in vogue. In ten years time it is possible that quite different views will prevail, with new findings in educational research.

Steiner by contrast was strongly of the opinion that the developing human being takes sudden leaps. Evidence for this can be found if we consider the initiation rituals of former cultures, which are here and there enjoying a revival.

In Waldorf schools, the transitions from kindergarten to Class 1, and from the lower to the upper school, are regarded as marking such phases, which embody a new stage of life that could, also, be celebrated. Passing into the upper school is marked by a farewell to the central figure of the class teacher who is replaced instead by various specialists. (This is true to some extent of the move to secondary school in the UK [at age 11/12], although in our view this happens too early.) Teachers at this level draw on the full competency of their specialist abilities and the desire to convey this to students. Their specialism is now called for and appropriate. It is a valuable experience for students to experience the authenticity of teachers who are fully committed to their fields.

But first and foremost the curriculum seeks to offer help to adolescents at a time of inner turbulence and the confusions of puberty. This can be done, for instance, in a main lesson on the history of revolutions; or also in literature lessons when, based on a reading of humorist texts, pupils learn to devise and enact various aspects of humour, with jokes or humorous turns of phrase. In mathematics, too, they discover how they can use their thinking to find a rapid solution to something which would take months to solve practically (as in issues of combinatorial analysis). Here they learn to balance the power of feelings, with which they are naturally endowed at this time, with the power of thinking.

In organic chemistry the students enter deeply and reflectively into processes involved in sugar, starch, cellulose, alcoholic fermentation and distillation, aerobic and anaerobic fermentation, the manufacture and properties of ether, esters and aromatic substances.

Physics engages with notions of heat and thermodynamics, and thus the mode of operation of the steam engine, the stirling motor and internal combustion engine (four-stroke, two-stroke, diesel engines, jet engines and rocket propulsion). This list alone can kindle interest in a world accessible to both boys and girls alike. At the same time it is very difficult if, due to GCSE strictures, such interesting subjects have either to be dispensed with entirely or reduced to the briefest outlines. Experience has shown that when proper time is taken for a subject then students discover an absorbing interest in the world, and this in turn lightens the troubles of puberty.

Class 10 is still to some degree marked by this period of puberty, but at some point midway through the year the sun of new-found reason breaks through, revealing a new assurance and self-assurance.

In literature now the students have a main lesson on metrics and poetics and are introduced to epic, lyric and dramatic forms, learning both to recognize and use these in their own writing. They meet the great works of English literature. Something rather remarkable happens in history: everything they learned in the lower school about ancient cultures is revisited, though now no longer in the form of pictures but in a wide-ranging cultural context. Both literature and history awaken in students what Goethe calls 'intuitively perceived judgement'. The great cultures of India, Persia, Mesopotamia, Egypt, China and Greece, the colonization campaigns of Alexander the Great, Greek philosophy and, in Nietzsche's phrase, the 'birth of tragedy', offer perspectives that embody the development of human consciousness.

Geography turns on the one hand to the earth's interior, to the lithosphere and plate tectonics, but also to the atmosphere around us and the stratosphere, with a corresponding study of meteorology (which offers a good opportunity for interesting sequences of observation). Chemistry addresses the anorganic realm, and mathematics brings a wealth of new competencies: quadratic equations, logarithms, laws for computing logarithms, and logarithmic scales in science. In geometry they study ways of handling the circle and straight line, trigonometry is introduced and, if there is enough time, representational or descriptive geometry. The land surveying practical is an important and characteristic aspect of Class 10: in measuring and surveying an area or region, pupils learn to apply triangulation in practice.

It is not a question of covering everything but of tapping in to the huge wealth of the curriculum and its diverse connection with the pupils' growth and development. Times have changed of course since Steiner's day. In the past Class 10 included a course in shorthand (!), a First Aid course, and a regular lesson in technology to ensure that pupils understood the equipment they would be using in life. Steiner suggested that we should understand the workings of every technology we ourselves use, at least in principle, in order to remain master of it and not its slave – a very understandable need in our current century.

Class 10 also practise art and crafts; and painting,

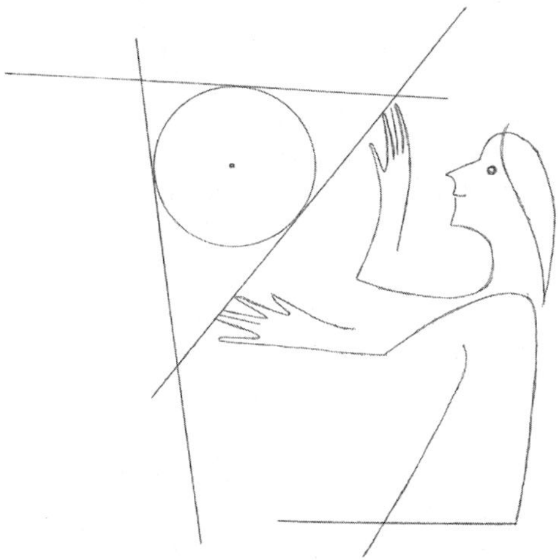

drawing, modelling and music continue to play an important part. The upper school choir (and if possible an orchestra) prepare their performances. And once again it seems almost incomprehensible that pupils and teachers manage to do all this in a single year. (Some schools even offer a forestry practical this year as well!)

In summary we can say that the Waldorf curriculum is a preparation for life and by its very nature is not simply geared to exams. There is a social obligation, of course, to enable students to take the exams they will need later. But from what has been said here it should be clear that this can impinge and negatively impact on the curriculum geared to the child's real developmental needs if the teaching group is not very attentive to this.

Class 11 and 12

In Class 11 and 12 the curriculum offers ever broader and comprehensive views of the world as students gradually reach the summit of their school learning.

Here is one example: in Class 11 the students study the great epic of *Parzival* by Wolfram von Eschenbach, a work of unfathomable depths. This gives them the chance to examine the laws at work in human biography, and at the same time to consider self-education and –development. If the 'innocent fool' is to become the 'Grail King' by the end of the narrative, his soul must undergo development and deprivations ordained by his 'higher self', embodied in its lower, distorted form in the character Kundry. Only thus can he achieve 'blessedness'.

And then comes world literature in Class 12: Dostoyevsky, Goethe, Tolstoy, Schiller, Handke, Emerson, Strindberg, Grass, Shakespeare, Racine, Hugo. In brief, literature offers its mighty panorama on the world and the human being.

The same is true, really, for all subjects. One pearl of the curriculum in Class 11 is the study of cartography, following on from geology in Class 9, and land surveying in Class 10. Here students learn to draw a map of the world with the correct mathematical and geometrical 'distortions' (projections due to the earth's curvature). In Class 12 all this is encompassed and surveyed once more in a main lesson that comprises economics, geography, ethnography and natural history. Likewise, in mathematics, a survey and conclusion is achieved by acquainting pupils with differential and integral calculus. Geometry is concerned with the development of vector geometry but finds a culmination in projective geometry. If there is time – unfortunately often not the case – mathematics can merge in a whole with astronomy and embryology as an all-encompassing conclusion.

In Chemistry pupils study the periodic table, but rather than offering this to them as a fixed grid they themselves investigate and discover it. 'It makes a great difference', says Frits Julius, 'whether one starts from the periodic system as a given or instead examines it as an important and remarkable discovery.' This is followed by a study of enzymes and hormones in biochemistry, leading us towards the human being – to immune response, and toxic effects on people and the natural world, as well as the search for a form of chemistry in harmony with the world and man. In chemistry, sustainability issues become existential.

Biology starts from embryology (and its correspondences with cosmology) to pass once again through all of zoology and, arriving back with the human being, to discuss modern ethical issues around reproductive and transplant medicine.

Often, at the end either of Class 11 or 12, pupils put on a large-scale drama production or a musical and also undertake a final art history trip together. It has become a tradition over the past 20 years to get students to finish their schooling with a special, individual project. A self-chosen theme is studied and presented to an audience. It is meant to have a theoretical aspect but also to involve practical implementation. One pupil studied the theory of ship-building, but also himself built a sailing dinghy (the class said: 'what an optimist!'). Another designed a costume for an opera role, delving into the psychology of the character, designing the costume accordingly, tailoring it and demonstrating what had gone into this work. A third designed a cash point machine that can be used by blind people and actually built the fronting for it. The range of examples is endless. There are also Waldorf schools where the whole class work on a final eurythmy performance project.

The curriculum reaches its culmination in Class 12 as an inherently artistic whole that is here rounded off and concluded, even if pupils continue learning for a lifetime. Class 13, which exists in some schools, serves solely for exam work and no longer draws on the Waldorf curriculum, even though, at the request of pupils, the hard slog of exam studies is relieved here and there with singing or eurythmy.

Recommended reading:

Avison, Kevin, and Martyn Rawson (2014). *The Tasks and Content of the Steiner-Waldorf Curriculum.* Edinburgh: Floris Books.

Lindenberg, Christoph (1989). *Teaching History: Suggested Themes for the Curriculum in Waldorf Schools.* Great Barrington, MA: AWSNA Publications.

Edelglass, Stephen (2006). *The Physics of Human Experience.* Hillsdale, NY: Adonis Press.

Gerwin, Douglas, ed. (2014). *Trailing Clouds of Glory: Essays on Human Sexuality and the Education of Youth in Waldorf Schools.* Chatham, NY: Waldorf Publications.

Greer, Anne (2010). *The Power of Grammar — A Phenomenological Approach.* Ghent, NY: AWSNA Publications.

Holdrege, Craig (2013). *Thinking Like a Plant: A Living Science for Life.* Great Barrington, MA: Lindisfarne Books.

Julius, Frits (2000). *Fundamentals for a Phenomenological Study of Chemistry.* Fair Oaks, CA: AWSNA Publications.

Kranich, Ernst-Michael (1999). *Thinking Beyond Darwin: The Idea of the Type as a Key to Vertibrate Evolution.* Hillsdale, NY: Adonis Press.

Ruef, Mona, ed. (2014). *Rubicon: Developmental Steps Ages 7-10 — Selections from the Works of Rudolf Steiner*. Chatham, NY: Waldorf Publications.

Sloan, David (2007). *Life Lessons: Reaching Teenagers through Literature.* Ghent, NY: AWSNA Publications.

Pedagogy

The Waldorf School is founded on a pedagogical approach formulated and devised by Rudolf Steiner (1861-1925) the initiator of anthroposophy, a term which can be interpreted, broadly, as 'awareness of our human nature'. This awareness, present in all, is usually asleep or semi-conscious and slumbering. Anthroposophy seeks to awaken it and to develop an ever fuller and richer sense of our humanity. In particular it offers a broader and deeper view of the human being and an awareness that there are no limits to consciousness but that the horizons of our perception and understanding can continually expand.

This broader view of the human being himself is not confined to our corporeal nature and psyche but sees a unique entelechy at work within us. This entelechy or individuality not only exists but also develops. Though present in the child it is as yet concealed; and the task of education is to unfold this hidden reality to the fullest possible extent. Just as a rose does not immediately blossom but a seed must first germinate and put forth stem, leaves and branches, eventually forming a calyx and then a flower, something similar is true of the child. He must grow and develop. His inner disposition is to unfold, flourish and blossom, or in other words eventually come to self-determination. But this growth needs its due time: as in the plant world so in us too.

It is highly characteristic of the human species that we cannot do this unaided but need the attention of others. We require education. To become autonomous and independent eventually we first need the other. As long as a child is young he needs help with almost everything in life. As he grows older, help and attention works by eliciting imitation in him, as we can see in the acquisition of speech, the 'mother tongue'. Smaller and greater skills arise in this way: dressing, washing, eating, drawing, relating and behaviour.

Only at play is the child fully himself, integrating imitated elements yet forming and building his own world with them. The capacities of standing, walking, speaking, listening and thinking are slowly consolidated, and basic hand skills develop. In other words, by the time of school readiness, around the age of 6 or 7, the child will have acquired a huge, albeit usually unconscious, repertoire of life skills. At school age different characteristics slowly emerge. Immediate imitation slowly comes to an end and is replaced by a more inward and intentional kind. The child wishes to imitate what others do. He wishes to learn but no longer so directly from life itself, more from another person to whom he entrusts himself. If this other deserves his love, the child will learn by natural inclination. We can regard this as devotion to a loved authority figure. (A child can also learn under compulsion or competitive pressure. In Waldorf schools this is not used as it is thought to be psychologically damaging.) The relationship with a beloved person, for whom a child is willing to learn things even if they are not always immediately gratifying, lasts for many years but also continually alters in nature. Increasingly as the child grows his talents or gifts start to emerge, but also his difficulties or limitations. Learning expands and diversifies hugely, and the teacher accompanies this process by growing too. The way she speaks to the children, and her learning strategies need to change to match the development of her pupils. Gradually her own understanding of them broadens and deepens. She is who she is of course, but she can change. She requires both flexibility and persistence.

And this is like a second form of imitation, in which children, who are now pupils, experience their teacher as accompanying, growing and learning alongside them – a model they too wish to emulate.

The next important stage in growth arrives at puberty (for which Steiner coined the lovely phrase 'earthly maturity') although today we should be clear that sexual maturity does not mean psychological maturity. Physical development is nowadays some years ahead of psychological.

The way that adults and teachers relate to young people changes radically now. Still confused about everything that is happening to him or her, the pupil meets teachers who do everything in their power to point the way into life, both through their own authentic identity and the specialist expertise and knowledge associated with it. If an adolescent has the good fortune to encounter such people at this age, in whom ability merges with honesty and self-reliance, a third and still more internalized phase of imitation can occur, expressed as pure enthusiasm for the being and capacities of an adult. This enthusiasm leads the adolescent out into the world and its significance. One does frequently meet people who were blessed by having teachers who stayed with them in their memory as significant figures.

In this phase of youth, the capacity to meet others awakens, and this gives encounters a whole new scope of importance which will be decisive for life. And then comes the moment when pupils enter life with a store of knowledge and ability, and a treasury of memories.

Applied pedagogy

To make this pedagogy a matter of practical application, teachers need a wealth of insights into the nature of the human being and his development, as described earlier. This helps them to understand the children and adolescents in their care. Of the wide range of insights that Steiner gave for understanding children, I will mention just a few here. It is easy to think, mistakenly, that these tools of perception could be used to pigeonhole or categorize a child. In fact this is not so. They are nothing more nor less than aids to understanding; and if teachers use them as such, this makes their contact with pupils better and easier – and this in turn is the foundation of all real education.

Temperament

One way to understand a pupil better is to recognize his temperament. In the simplest terms, one can distinguish more active, energetic children (choleric), more lively and communicative children (sanguine), more thorough and persistent (phlegmatic) and more introverted children (melancholic). Usually, though, two temperaments will predominate in a child, with one more prominent than the other. These temperamental hues can also alter as the years pass.

Recognizing the temperament of a child is a first step. The second is to engage with him in a way that addresses and draws on it. This is the beginning of the real art of education. When speaking to children we fully accept the character of each and learn to address their diverse nuances of temperament in the way we speak, say, or do arithmetic, tell stories to them or allocate tasks in grammar. This will enliven things in the classroom and help to give children the sense that they are understood. Ultimately this also helps a teacher to recognize and balance her own temperament, with its positive aspects and drawbacks.

Constitution

It is very useful to try to discern whether a pupil – or also the teacher herself – tends more to a disposition coloured by intellect, feeling or action. A child who largely 'lives in his head' needs to be addressed dif-

ferently from one who lives more in feelings; and differently again from one who only really feels engaged when he has something to do.

We can get a sense of which of three systems prevails (neuro-sensory, rhythmic or limb system) already in the child's outward appearance. Having detected this we can then engage with a one-sided quality and try to balance it over a longer period. Again, this is educational artistry which really oils the workings of our relationships with pupils.

Mode of thinking

We can observe pupils (and ourselves) to see how we think. This is not necessarily anything to do with intelligence but only with the *mode* of thinking. Is this more conceptual and analytic, or more pictorial and bound to context? The importance of such reflections quickly becomes apparent. If I, as a teacher, am very conceptual in my mode of thinking and encounter a pupil who thinks in pictures and more tangible connections, this will easily lead to misunderstandings. A teacher might think a pupil is 'unintelligent' simply because he thinks in a different way. To form a picture oneself of the kind of thinking a child intrinsically employs can be very helpful for pupil-teacher communication. (This is also a problem that can arise if teachers with a pronounced expertise in teaching upper school children suddenly have to teach young ones.)

Imagination

We all have inner mental pictures. In some of us these remain bound to what we relate to directly while in others they begin to lead an independent life of their own, becoming the power of imagination. We all have some imaginative capacity and children do especially, living strongly in imagination in their play for instance. Play is a serious activity for them. Some children show a vivid and lively imagination while others are more prosaic and down-to-earth. Children who have a strong imaginative life may often not be able to keep it at arm's length but can be dominated by their inner pictures.

In the normal school day, for instance, one may see Class 3 children who start playing a particular game the moment break-time comes, while others stand by and watch. In Class 6, when it is time to write something, some will look worriedly at the blank piece of paper while others fill page after page.

Here again we must acknowledge the differences between children and, in each situation, lead them towards new capacities. The attention of more imaginative ones can be drawn to more mundane matters while those less so can be led towards aesthetic appreciation. Are we aware of our own disposition here? How does this play into the way we relate to pupils? For instance, do we have the ability to imagine what it would feel like to be inside the skin of a particular child? If so, how would we experience ourselves as the teacher?

Teachers need their powers of imagination in all

kinds of situation, for instance also if a child does something he shouldn't. Imaginative engagement with smaller or greater transgressions during the school day, and not just reacting with the standard moral indignation, will make school life more creatively alive for all.

Interests

As children grow older, their gifts and interests become visible (although of course very marked gifts can appear earlier). Children have many interests but a particular tendency is always present: either they are drawn more to idealism (I want to be a famous conductor) or in a more mundane direction (I'm going to earn lots of money and drive a big car). The latter example is likely to figure in earlier childhood, and by Class 6 and 7 this will take on a different cast: one pupil may immerse himself in the world of animals while another becomes a computer geek.

We are less concerned with value judgements here than with the kind of focus. What are a person's interests? What do they get enthusiastic about? One person acquires encyclopaedic knowledge about aeroplanes while another wants to save the oceans from plastic waste. For one, philosophy is the be-all and end-all, for another it is stock market fluctuations. Some really love artistic activity while others prefer a walk or a glass of beer. One person likes movies, the other prefers museums. One writes poems – in secret – in his free time, while the other – also in secret – has spent years building up his model railway at home. All these are fully justified. Our interests show what kind of person we are.

Interests also show gender starting to play a role. Obsession with horses in Class 6 is something one sees more amongst girls, whereas computer geeks are almost all boys. The distinctive nature of the female or male constitution start to come to the fore here.

Steiner sharply criticized the pedagogical exploitation of a gift in choosing a profession (e.g. that a pupil should study mathematics because he is very good at maths). He believed that a school should not force a pupil in a particular direction dictated by his abilities. It was quite possible, he thought, that someone with a great, and perhaps one-sided mathematical gift ought *not* to become a mathematician, since this was an ability he already possessed. The reverse might also be true: someone discovers a great love for a subject at school, and wants to study it at university; and then no one would wish to stand in the way of this enthusiasm. The general rule here is therefore: a child's gifts can but should not have to determine his further education and future.

Our interests are mysterious in origin. Where do they come from? They are no doubt partly determined by sociological and genetic factors and have something to do with a child's constitution. Yet that is not the whole answer. Why does one girl continually want to play chess? Or how does another know at the age of 16 that she wants to study sinology, and then goes ahead and does so?

Interests can embody an unconscious, deeply hidden impulse, as if a person is led towards a type of profession or future career.

We can see that two great realities can inform and guide the destiny of upper school pupils: the school's support for a particular area of interest (through the wide-ranging curriculum), and human encounter between children and adults. In the view of the Waldorf School, adolescents therefore have the right to a *rich, unhurried general education.*

Thinking versus will

We all know situations when we need to find a solution of some kind; and we have all experienced times when solutions, for good or ill, were easier or more difficult to carry out. Some people can make decisions much more easily than others, for whom they can start to seem like an insurmountable task. Is the path that leads from intention to realization a direct one, or are there hindrances that intervene?

These questions touch on a person's (potential) integrity. The Waldorf School tries to educate its pupils to enable them as adults to realize an insight through corresponding actions. Can education lead people to do 'what is right' quite naturally? Waldorf education strives for this, but not by intellectual instruction or moral precept since this only very rarely really alters outlook and behaviour. Developing a person's (future) self-assurance and willpower is a core aspect of its approach. It attempts to prepare this future integrity by artistic means, assuming that all artistic activity 'integrates the upper and lower poles'. These apt expressions, drawn from anthroposophy, are a way to understand the difference between insight and realization of it. Integrity of the personality is made possible by this artistic and dynamic interaction between the poles of thinking and will. However, few concepts can be so easily misunderstood as 'artistic teaching', even within the Waldorf world itself. In the next section we will explore this further.

The religious sensibility

In his treatise on politics and education, Gert Biesta states that in his view schooling has three functions: development of skills, socialization and, as he paraphrases it, 'subjectification' (establishing secure self-awareness). In anthroposophic terms we would call this 'I development'. He ascertains that where education and teaching are state-run, state-funded and subject to state responsibility, education increasingly focuses on skill development, which can be tested and checked.

Yet he regards socialization and self-awareness as education's real tasks, since these constitute lasting 'inner values'. This is a very helpful point of view. If learning is not seen only as the acquisition of skills but as a path of gradually increasing engagement with the world and human community, then learning has a connecting quality. If education really encompasses all these three areas it has a religious tenor also. Everything connected with the will to learn, respect for others and the world, interest, wonder and enthusiasm, awakens this kind of non-confessional religiosity. In Waldorf schools one can perceive this as a quiet undertone – a diffuse but real sense of underlying religiosity.

Naturally schools will also offer proper 'religious education' at parents' request, and in accordance with their respective religious beliefs. Non-denominational religion lessons are also often provided in the curriculum: broadly Christian-based, these touch on issues of concern to the children and cultivate a religious sense of things without pinning this to any belief system. Such lessons may, for instance, include biographies of inspiring historical and contemporary figures, whether or not they themselves had religious convictions.

Recommended reading:

Biesta, Gert (2012): 'Good education in an age of measurement; on the need to reconnect with the question of purpose in education.' University of Stirling, London, UK.

Biesta, Gert, (2014): 'The beautiful risk of Education', University of Stirling, London, UK.

Teaching Artistically

The following four realms where art informs education can help us understand the concept of an artistic approach to teaching.

1. Teachers and their personal relationship to art
2. The use of art in lessons
3. The art of education
4. Aesthetics

The third point above is clearly key when we speak of 'artistic teaching'. Yet further distinctions are needed here since artistic teaching means something different for a games teacher, a kindergarten teacher or a chemistry or language teacher.

Teachers and their personal relationship to art

In his original suggestions to (at that time future) teachers, Steiner placed great emphasis on their practice of art in some form. It will be difficult for a teacher to achieve the previously mentioned integrity of upper and lower poles if she does not have a sound basis for this in her own experience. This was also why Steiner formulated the key principle that 'education is always self-education'.

Those wishing to become teachers of this kind will need to discover some degree of artistic flair in themselves. Having an innate artistic sense helps our relationships with others, with children and colleagues, run more smoothly. It stimulates the imagination and helps us be inventive in the classroom. Some are more drawn to pictorial art, others to music or drama. Depending on inclination or disposition, a future teacher will find an artistic domain to develop. And this also is a self-renewing and life-enhancing activity to keep us fresh and open.

Using art in lessons

As strange as it may sound, painting, drawing and modelling, for example, are *not* the essence of the Waldorf School, despite being an important characteristic of it. A neat and well-presented main lesson book is an important integrative process for pupils, and a means by which they not only learn but realize and embody their learning. This simple example illustrates the effect of integrating the 'upper' (thinking) and 'lower' pole (will) so that the main lesson book becomes part of a holistic approach involving both cognitive skills and activity.

When pupils engage in ever more complex form drawings, this helps them develop their visual powers and design skills. Painting enables them to express moods in colour, and without doubt it creates an inner capacity to experience life in a more vivid and qualitative way. They become more receptive to inner and outer impressions. Something similar could be said for all artistic activities.

A common criticism of Waldorf schools is that they always resort to the same artistic styles which inhibit free artistic development and expression. In terms of the 'finished product' this may be understandable but here we are far less concerned with the outcome than with the process and experience involved. (However, in the higher classes, especially, very individual and beautiful works and artefacts are often produced. And even in lower classes, despite common traits of style and medium, anyone who knows the children will invariably find a distinctive quality in each child's painting.) A detached observer may look at paintings on a classroom wall and see in them many repetitions of the same. This fails however to discern the artistic activity itself, the experience that went in to creating them. Ultimately, art also depends on skill and proper handling of materials. No one would dream of looking askance at a hopeful pianist practising scales.

Another criticism concerns the relationship between art and learning in the upper school. And it is true that upper school pupils themselves can suffer from 'too much art' if the teaching faculty does not ensure a proper balance between intellectual demands and artistic activity. This balance can also be assured by greater individualization in the range of artistic activity offered in the upper school.

The art of education

This is the core of this pedagogy. It means a form of teaching that breathes, pulsing between concentration and relaxation, between intensive listening and independent activity; that passes through intensifying phases, approaching the theme, presenting it, then deepening it. Related themes are added, then moments too of reflection. Independent work alternates with group activity. In brief, this kind of teaching resembles a process of breathing.

In a way this has an affinity with sonata form in music: first the theme is presented (exposition), then developed and led into an intensified repetition (reprise) before its summation and conclusion (coda). It is not exaggerated to compare the form of a successful lesson with the laws of musical form. In later school years the conclusion will come the next day and lead to a conceptualization of the teaching material.

A teacher who 'composes' her lessons in this way can be called a 'teaching artist'. Lessons are not built up according to a fixed schema or rigid sequence but have a dynamic or musical form, and this in turn conveys an experience of time that is not so much linear as elastic and dynamic. This is also why the beginning of a lesson is so important: can the pupils sense that something is in the air, or will it just be 'business as usual'? Much depends on this. If the children intimate that something is coming, they do not yet know what – that it is approaching them and will soon become apparent, the whole lesson will have a quite different atmosphere from teaching which simply goes through the usual motions. These are the conditions for a form of teaching with inner momentum, and it is in this sense that we can speak of the teacher as an artist.

One effect of a form of teaching that breathes like this is that questions of discipline recede into the background. The pupils experience themselves as being buoyed up in a current of meaning. If the teacher has also become accustomed to seeing every individual in a class and not just the group en masse, so that individual relationships develop, an ideal foundation for this art of teaching is created.

These are ideal descriptions of course. But it seems important to highlight the ideal so as to focus clearly on what we are trying to do and allow the nature of teaching as an art to emerge as fully as possible. People may regard such ideals as too lofty. But I would counter this by saying that while artistic teaching does indeed require ability, it depends still more on stance and outlook, and a commitment to these. One of these basic stances – and pupils immediately notice if it is there or not – is enthusiasm. In the Waldorf School nothing can work without a grounded and grounding enthusiasm.

Aesthetics

To end this chapter let us touch on the fourth aspect of art. As described elsewhere in this book, we can regard it as a right of children to grow up in an aesthetically pleasing environment. In their formative years, after all, pupils spend a great deal of time in the same surroundings; and the form and colour of these surroundings, the 'gesture' inherent in a building, engrave themselves deeply into their unconscious memory and sensibility and can create a fundamental mood of soul that accompanies them for the rest of their lives.

Here it is less significant whether the well cared-for and beautiful surroundings in which teaching takes place correspond to *our own* aesthetic ideals. It is far more important whether these surroundings can actually aesthetically imbue and inform children.

At the interface between art and craft, Waldorf schools have developed important innovations. This began with the Hibernia School initiated by Klaus Fintelmann in Wanne-Eickel, Germany. This school's founder and creator was deeply convinced that intellectual education must go hand in hand with craft and handwork skills. Many generations of children have passed through this school, leaving with their exam certificates in one hand, as it were, and in the other hand a completed apprenticeship in, say, metalwork. A number of other Waldorf schools have adopted this idea in some form or other, and in many of them vocational training runs alongside other schoolwork. There are also still Waldorf schools with large workshops where pupils can undertake craft projects and complete commissions alongside normal lessons.

Technology and Education

Not so long ago a joke was going the rounds amongst Waldorf parents that when the classteacher comes for a visit you should cover up the TV with a tablecloth and say, 'We don't watch television!' Traditionally the Waldorf School has been regarded as somewhat anti-technology. The truth is that Waldorf teachers try to be aware of the role technology can and ought to play in education. Technology as a curriculum subject also invites such reflections.

Broadly these considerations lead to the following outcome: we attempt to introduce technology and its use in a way that enables the user (in this case the pupil) to remain master of any appliance as far as possible rather than developing a dependency on it. Further study would be needed to see how far this aim is realized – not an easy matter since the world of technology, especially electronic media, is changing so rapidly. At the beginning of 2014 it was already being predicted that the social media sites Facebook and Twitter would soon be a thing of the past and would be superseded at any moment by Whatsapp.

In relation to these issues we can identify two extreme stances: one opposes these technological advances, seeking to 'protect' pupils from them, while the other embraces them unequivocally. The first can be seen in American Waldorf schools, where parents are actually asked to limit children's use of electronic media, and this forms part of the home-school agreement. The second view is apparent in Dutch Waldorf schools where electronic media are integrated into school life and form part of the interactions between school and pupils.

Waldorf schools are not intrinsically anti-technology, but they do reflect on these issues, exploring the right balance between modernity and health. Education is never arbitrary – everything we do with and for children will eventually have an effect of some kind.

That these schools are right to be cautious is apparent from studies such as those by Manfred Spitzer. Entitled, for instance, 'Digital Dementia' and 'Screen Danger', these publications show, interestingly, that academics are far more aware of the effect of electronic media than these media themselves are willing to concede to the general public. Nowadays schools are tasked with ensuring pupils develop 'media competency'. But such competency is only effective if mere information is developed into the skill (competency) to handle these technologies fully and remain aware both of their scope and their limitations. Simply teaching computer skills can sometimes lead to the opposite of this.

In some Waldorf schools computer lessons start with pupils learning, in both maths and technology, what underlies computer language and programming. Some schools even get their ninth graders soldering circuit boards to add and subtract with. The aim here is to gain some basic understanding at least of what goes on in the computer's 'black box'. It is typical of the Waldorf approach to seek to know how something functions.

It is a school's task to make no concessions whatever to addictive behaviour. Usually the word 'addiction' suggests substance dependency (alcohol or drugs), and we may forget that habits of other kinds can become addictive too. All sorts of addictive habits are increasing today, and the key question here is always, 'Who is controlling whom?'

Human-scale engagement with technology and the avoidance of addiction is something Waldorf schools aspire to. The extent to which they succeed in this will depend also on how far it is possible to work with parents in this realm.

Recommended reading:

Martin Large, *Who's Bringing Them Up?* Hawthorn Press 1990.

Buzzell, Keith (1998). *The Children of Cyclops: The Influence of Television Viewing on the Developing Human Brain.* Fair Oaks, CA: AWSNA Publications.

Cordes, Colleen, and Edward Miller, eds. (2000). *Fool's Gold: A Critical Look at Computers in Childhood.* College Park, MD: Alliance for Childhood.

Sources

The art of Waldorf education emerged from the genius of Rudolf Steiner. Educationalists have picked up on many of its innovative approaches but it has to be said that education in general has not implemented radical reforms. Instead, an emphasis has developed on results and outcomes in education but without any real concern for the laws of child development. An achievement-oriented society creates schools geared to achievement. Waldorf education dares to question such assumptions.

Academic critics of Waldorf education (of whom there are few) have been fair in their assessment of this. The Waldorf School so far remains the only genuinely new educational model for the whole age-range from kindergarten through to school-leaving age, and is represented in 56 countries of the world. It draws on the art of education as Steiner formulated it in countless lectures he gave between 1902 and 1924, which later provided the foundation for the work of the first Waldorf school in Stuttgart. Its underlying principles are rooted in anthroposophy, which among other things, sees the human being and human life in far broader terms than normal, and seeks to enquire into basic questions of existence – for instance, where we come from and where we are going. Steiner points to ways in which we can broaden our view of life to include pre-birth and after-death existence, an entirely self-evident concern not so long ago for philosophers of the German Idealist school. The idea of reincarnation, for instance, is explored by authors such as Lessing, Schelling, Goethe and Herder.

Views of pre-birth and after-death existence are commonly regarded today as the domain of religious doctrine, and a matter of faith. But independent intellectual enquiry can allow us to examine such ideas for ourselves and ask if they are conceivable. Is there a way to test the evidence for ourselves and enquire into such ideas by our own means?

In his lifetime Steiner always hoped that the scientific community would give serious attention to his research in the spiritual domain, and recognize how his findings could complement the mainstream view. But he was forced to acknowledge that there was no willingness to engage in this realm. The sciences secluded themselves behind the narrow doors of their disciplines, and basically this remains true today.

Like other key figures of the 20th century such as the General Secretary of the United nations Dag Hammerskjoeld, we can see Steiner as a modern initiate. Both men developed vision of the world of primal forces and origins, and could describe this in the light of their modern consciousness. Steiner's cosmogony offers a vast panorama which may sound like a fairytale to those who do not have his faculties: a tale of mighty connections and confluences of meaning, highly rewarding for many who long to free themselves from the narrow bounds of a merely materialistic outlook.

Anthroposophy is by no means at odds with a scientific view, but merely considers that this outlook is not in itself sufficient for explaining the phenomena and riddles of the world. It offers ways of perceiving, knowing and describing the other necessary half of reality, giving rise to a view of the human being that goes beyond merely visible or measurable factors, and penetrating to an emergent 'life' principle within us. As we can see from a careful study of physiology, life is and still remains a mystery inaccessible to a merely scientific mode of enquiry. (In fact science itself ought to acknowledge the gap here in its own knowledge and models of understanding.)

The same is true of questions about human interiority, of the soul. If we were only a brilliant biochemical reactor, would life or human biography have any meaning? If love is only a matter of raging hormones, devoid of a spiritual aspect, what is the point of empathy, real charity, sympathy and happiness? And why do we try to shape our lives in the way we feel accords with us? This can only have significance if we also have a spiritual identity, continuous with an existence before birth and after death, for ultimately this embeds our life and actions in a whole, broader context of meaning.

With these questions we touch on the idea of the fourfold human being, who lives in a body on earth and bears the life principle within him. Into this living entity is integrated an experiencing, learning, develop-

ing soul; and all this is encompassed in our spiritual individuality or I.

Development of these four levels or aspects of the human being does not occur simultaneously. In early childhood development is predominantly of the body and life functions, only after which inner or soul development comes into its own. It can never emerge before bodily development has first given it sure foundations. A longer period is then needed before we come into a sense of our own identity as a self-determining person, which tends to happen at the end of the second decade. This is like a developing plant, which has to take its time to grow before a flower and seeds emerge. Grains of corn do not appear or ripen quicker if we tug hard at them: they abide by their own inner laws. If we regard human development in this light, we can draw certain conclusions from it for a human-scale and child-centred pedagogy.

But this also means that the non-sensory realm is not nothing merely because invisible, but is filled with meaning, purpose and reality. Anthroposophy and the art of education founded on it, seek integration of both these worlds, the sensory and non-sensory, in the conviction that the quality of human life will be all the better for inclusion of this other perspective. This definitely does *not* mean that these insights into human nature should be taught to pupils, or that parents should be urged to 'accept' them on faith. This is certainly not the aim. Instead anthroposophy and the art of education provide inspiration for increasing the quality of education, which in our view is paramount. The remarkable thing is that educationalists nowadays acknowledge that an education which conveys only functional knowledge and information is not what growing children need; and yet they have not yet really found practical measures and proposals to bring such change about. It is to be hoped that some debate at least can continue between more traditional educational approaches and the really innovative Waldorf approach.

This enlarged and broadened view of the nature of human existence is reflected among other things in an attention to laws and patterns at work in human development, which are subsequently applied in both teaching methodology and the curriculum. These both seek to reflect and respond to the child's changing developmental requirements. Archetypal in character, these laws are nevertheless formulated in an open-ended way to allow continuing revision and elaboration. There are a great many publications by Waldorf practitioners worldwide which have further enlarged on the original curriculum with new ideas and developments. There is a continuous stream of research into pedagogy, methodology and curriculum, and empirical studies on Waldorf education and its practice are also being undertaken.

Nevertheless, it has taken a long time to address an obstinate misunderstanding – that Waldorf schools are 'schools for anthroposophists'. Ultimately this misapprehension was cleared up by the above-mentioned empirical studies on the effectiveness of this form of education. The Church too (in the narrower sectarian sense) has never been quick to correct misinterpretations and false statements about others, and found it hard to accept that an idea arising from the spirit of anthroposophy could in fact – as was clearly shown – nurture generally human qualities such as tolerance, interest, social adjustment and self-determination.

Modern Challenges and Future Demands

As already emphasized, the account of Waldorf educational practice presented here tries to clearly show what 'Waldorf' really means and what it doesn't. It is also true to say, however, that every school is only as good as its teachers. Steiner's art of education makes high, though attainable demands. Sometimes pupils or parents turn away from the Waldorf School in disappointment, feeling that the ideals they sought when they approached the school have not been fulfilled, or have been overlaid by negative experiences: a sense perhaps that expectations and ideals are set too low, or that daily reality simply does not accord with the stated aims or 'ideology'. Yet if this new educational paradigm were only an ideology, it would be high time to abolish it. In fact the idea at the heart of this schooling is an ideal in the sense that it is only justified by actual, successful practice. This is the *only* decisive factor. The theory is only valid in so far as it bears real fruit. And so we have to ask whether these schools lead pupils into life in a way that gives them a sustaining educational experience and also nurtures rather than harming their health. Do the schools practise a methodology that really cultivates pupils' capacities and potential? Do they develop children's interest in others and the world, leading eventually to real social skills and the capacity to lead one's life in a self-reliant way? These are the important criteria which ultimately constitute the value of a school. However, there are certain hindrances today which can get in the way of this.

External challenges

A current global trend is to limit all education to the full development of just a few skills and capacities, giving rise to an ever narrower 'performance' spiral. The PISA tests are a classic example of this. No one considers asking, any more, whether such achievements really serve the needs of the children who have to produce them. Some schools drill their pupils in PISA tests to produce good results. This has little to do with real learning, since anything learned in this way will vanish like the morning mist. We are becoming increasingly a 'knowledge-based society' and yet in real life most professions require actual skills and expertise rather than theoretical knowledge alone.

Here, as in almost everything else, the Waldorf schools take a different stance. Their abiding concern instead is the wellbeing and individual development of a growing human being, and they stay true to this through every passing educational fashion.

Sometimes this sense of always swimming against the prevailing tide can be felt as tiring: it would be easier to work within a context of understanding. And yet this is simply the fate of a pedagogy which seeks new approaches. We could even say that the Waldorf School is trying to establish a new paradigm in education that reconciles learning with personal development.

The relationship between state and school

The Waldorf schools view their work as serving civil society: independent, responsible people (parents) seek a particular type of education for their children. The state in Britain allows this in the form of self-financing 'independent schools' or, more recently, state-funded 'academies', though in the latter case the state exercises more control and there is an ongoing debate within the Waldorf movement as to whether state funding may curb and limit 'Waldorf' approaches. Here, therefore, Waldorf schools are balanced perilously between an independent education available largely to wealthier classes and a state-funded model with some limits on the full scope of independence.

Exams and tests

The Waldorf School cannot be opposed to exams in principle, since the whole of life consists in trials and tests of some kind or other. But by increasingly determining the content and nature of exams, and making these ever more prescriptive, the state can have very constraining effects on the Steiner-Waldorf curriculum. Based very much on the idea of development, this curriculum cannot simply be pushed to one side as exams approach without endangering the school's identity. This would also mean that upper school teaching might increasingly become geared to ensuring good exam results instead of focusing on what pupils really need: content that wakens their interest, giving them a means to understand the world and nurturing their individualization. This problem can be resolved but it requires the school to have, on the one hand, a strong sense of its real task, and on the other the energy, courage and imagination to reconcile the irreconcilable.

Some schools are experimenting with project-based exams. At the same time a group of colleagues is trying to develop specifically Waldorf school-leaving qualifications that would be recognized for university entry, similar to the International Baccalaureat. In Switzerland the exam problem has been solved with a now accepted Waldorf qualification which largely safeguards the Steiner curriculum. However, most schools still fulfil their task for society by offering mainstream exams, trying to integrate the preparation for these into daily school life in as reasonable a way as possible – with inevitably associated risks to the curriculum.

Internal challenges

Structure and impulse

An ideal can only be realized if it finds a corresponding vessel and structure in which to live and develop. Otherwise it remains only an idea. Increasingly 'form' takes precedence over idea in the world, leading to a preoccupation with structure and organization. Thus many questions of inner content are replaced or 'answered' through such structures. There is a protocol, a 'policy' or fixed guideline to determine everything, and this leads to an over-structuring of all areas of society. We can see this in politics, insurance, the health service, the economy, in education and in many other domains. The same trend can be discerned in Waldorf schools in over-determination of daily practice, associated inevitably with ever-increasing bureaucracy. But real pedagogy needs free scope for decision, action and form. Where this scope is too greatly constrained by fixed regulations, pedagogy itself can suffocate. These regulations and 'guidelines' exert a rigidifying effect on school life. It is important that idea, impulse and form develop the right mutual relationship to facilitate enough freedom in the teachers' work, and that the forms established can always allow expression of underlying ideals. This balance creates the air in which pedagogy can breathe. Where it is not found, a school is very likely to develop rigid and dogmatic forms of conduct, leading more or less inevitably to barriers with the outside world. Dogmatism and sectarianism are completely alien to the spirit of the Waldorf School. The balance referred to is particularly important in education which depends on developing a certain reliable predictability. Good habits are a blessing in daily teaching practice but they need conscious nurturing, and where this is lacking habits can come to plague us. Where the teaching day is over-informed by fixed 'rituals' there is a danger of routine replacing creativity. It is important that we keep asking why and how we work rather than basking too comfortably in familiarity.

Randomness

Everything to do with anthroposophy is founded on freedom, and therefore every teacher is free to take up or reject what she decides to. This presents a challenge too: anthroposophic ideas are not a closed system of actions that should be adhered to but are invariably embodied in each person's own insights. Yet this can lead to arbitrariness, which is, again, at odds with the spirit of Waldorf education. The wide and creative diversity of teachers' practice always has to find its justification in real, anthroposophically-founded perceptions of the children's needs. A more random approach can start to rear its head in seemingly harmless phrases such as 'I see things differently' or 'I have a different view on this'; or also often, 'we live in a different time now'. It is a delicate balance to find one's own authentic view and yet keep relating this to the school's shared understanding of its task. While it is certainly true that we now live in a different era, we still need to ask whether being 'modern' is the same as really answering contemporary needs – by which I mean finding the right action at the right moment.

Stuck in a rut

One hopes that children will experience a school environment that is anything other than 'staid': that is alive, full of varied activity, where there is room for refreshing ideas, real encounters and exciting perspectives. It is however all too easy for daily school life to become routine and dully predictable. Then one school day looks like any other; pupils and teachers relate to each other as required yet somehow there is a greyness about it, likewise between teachers and parents. A side effect of this atmosphere is that it impedes transparency, instead allowing invisible and disagreeable power structures to develop, with much 'collateral damage': parents often feel frustrated or even incensed, and yet feel impotent to alter anything.

All of us begin each new day with a secret question about what it may bring. Will the day be worth our effort? Consciously or unconsciously we also look back each evening and judge how the day went. Was it worth having? These are the thoughts of an adult, but how often do we read in the faces of children hurrying to school any happy expectancy of what is to come? It is childlike in the best sense to look forward to the day ahead. And wonderful affirmation of a school if its children go home satisfied by their experiences at the end of the day.

The social task

Let's say someone wishes to become a baker. He or she undergoes the training necessary for this, and then comes the moment to embark on this career. The freshly baked baker borrows money and opens a bakery. He bakes his bread as he's meant to, but also in accordance with his own ideas about what makes a good loaf. The work is varied and grows, and then the baker has to look around for staff to serve customers or to help with the baking. The bakery thrives for the bread is excellent, and the staff friendly. All goes well. The bakery grows in size and the baker has to deal with related matters such as shop design, accounts and increasing his product range. Later, when the business is employing more than ten staff, he appoints a half-time accounts manager. Then he joins an independent bakers' association, where he can get and share ideas about running his business more efficiently. He adopts measures he thinks fit his business but he remains in charge of his shop and responsible for the bread that is baked there, even if he starts delegating some of this responsibility to others.

That is one picture. Now here is another.

Someone wishes to become a baker. He or she undergoes the necessary training and then comes the moment to embark on this career. The freshly baked baker turns to a large bakery enterprise which gives him a job and, since his work is excellent, appoints him to a branch where he becomes manager. Business thrives but he has no say about the bread which he sells. All he does is bake the products delivered to him for baking. The business itself is run by specialists who take care of all 120 branches of the enterprise. They tastefully arrange his shop window, changing it through the year. Accounts are also managed by headquarters, as is the range of products.

There is no value judgement in these two examples, for a large-scale enterprise can also produce excellent bread. But they are useful as an illustration of Steiner's approach to the idea of *self-administration*. The first is a very simple and common form of it. It could be said that bread is so important for human beings that it should only be baked by those who can take direct responsibility for it. (In this example the independent baker stands for the school faculty or college.) Steiner did indeed believe that education was of such importance that it should only be practised by those who took direct responsibility for it. Such responsibility ought not to be anonymized by industry diktats or politicians whose priorities might lie elsewhere entirely than in education; even if education is their priority, they are likely to expect the same 'product' from every branch.

In brief, Steiner connected the idea of a new form of education with the idea of a new form of administration, or rather self-administration. He thought that those who wished to work in such a school should gradually also become responsible for everything that arises there, just as the baker is responsible for the whole 'profile' of his business, and especially the quality of his bread. It would be easy to think this applies too to all the social professions involved in helping or supporting fellow human beings. Other professions can be run differently of course – say production plants for producing technical equipment.

The history of the founding of the Waldorf School shows that basically this was Steiner's sole proposal for school organization: the fundamental idea of self-administration and the setting up of a teachers' faculty that would hold a pedagogical meeting once a week, along with a management meeting to administer the school. This management meeting appoints a manager and administrative staff.

There are Waldorf schools organized like this, but others which have a more differentiated structure; and others again which have relinquished this form of self-administration and appoint a non-pedagogical school management. In other words, there is a broad diversity of organizational forms to be found.

The form of management and administration suitable for one school can only be found by that particular school itself, since every school is different. Schools that reach a certain age or size often have to review and revise their organizational structures.

The resulting problems can also explain why schools sometimes seek external advisers. Many school communities feel they are not able to establish a form that is suitable for them. Especially in schools that may now be a generation old, questions about the right organizational form can give rise to various forms of upheaval or restlessness. This is like certain animals which at some point in their life cycle have to shed a skin or cast their antlers so that something new can grow.

Conclusion

Despite inevitable inadequacies that arise in a 'work in progress', Waldorf schools deserve a great deal of recognition for the courage they show in pursuing their own paths and swimming against the flow. Their capacity to keep questioning what they do is cause for admiration. They are, after all, the only type of school that seeks to realize Steiner's art of education. It is to be hoped that these pages have shown the value of attempting and practising this.

It is certainly not easy to find middle ways between randomness and persistence, between adaptation and renewal, and between individualism and community. But these schools are in dynamic development. They are on the move; and those who take their own steps are less likely to be compelled in directions dictated by others.

These schools vary greatly from country to country, and must adapt to different governmental requirements. Nevertheless, as a diverse yet united movement they are making a really important contribution to renewal in the education system. They persevere in the attempt to offer the next generation a sustaining form of education, helping it to become self-determining within a truly social context. Where this succeeds, young people find their own resources of intellectual creativity and can solve the problems they encounter. In other words, they can shape their own lives.

What could be better than to participate in such a venture?